DATE DUE

NOV 2 7 2000	
DEC 1 8 2000	

DEMCO INC 38-2971

Muslim Women

Muslim Women

Crafting a North American Identity

Shahnaz Khan

University Press of Florida

Gainesville/Tallahassee/Tampa/Boca Raton

Pensacola/Orlando/Miami/Jacksonville

The interviews with Iram and Karima in chapter 4 were previously published
in "Muslim Women: Negotiations in the Third Space" by Shahnaz Khan
in *Signs*, vol. 23, no. 2. Copyright 1998 by the University of Chicago.
All rights reserved. Reprinted with permission.

The interviews with Zubaida in chapter 3 and with Zahra and Nabia in
chapter 4 were previously published in "Situating Muslim Women's
Narratives" by Shahnaz Khan in the journal *Legal Studies Forum,*
vol. 21, no. 4, 1997. Reprinted with permission.

Printed in the United States of America on acid-free paper

05   04   03   02   01   00   6   5   4   3   2   1

Library of Congress Cataloging-in-Publication Data
Khan, Shahnaz.
Muslim women: crafting a North American identity / Shahnaz Khan.
p. cm.
Includes bibliographical references and index.
ISBN 0-8130-1749-1 (alk. paper)
1. Muslim women—Ontario—Toronto Metropolitan Area—Interviews.
2. Women immigrants—Ontario—Toronto Metropolitan Area—Interviews.
3. Women—Ontario—Toronto Metropolitan Area—Identity—Case studies. I. Title.
HQ1460.T63 K53 2000
305.48'69710713541—dc   99-059749

The University Press of Florida is the scholarly publishing agency for the State
University System of Florida, comprising Florida A&M University, Florida
Atlantic University, Florida International University, Florida State University,
University of Central Florida, University of Florida, University of North
Florida, University of South Florida, and University of West Florida.

University Press of Florida
15 Northwest 15th Street
Gainesville, FL 32611–2079
http://www.upf.com

To Apa, Zohra, Zainab, and Raza

CONTENTS

INTRODUCTION

Muslim Women: Crafting a North American Identity explores the multiple determinations of Muslim female identity—in particular, how individual women appear averse to either coding themselves as Muslim or allowing others to code them as such. Indeed, some of the statements of women whom I interviewed for this study suggest a distancing, a dislike, as they turn away from identifying themselves as Muslim. Yet their narratives also hint at a nostalgia and a longing for a stable and comfortable identity. They desire to be Muslim. In this book I examine the politics of this contradictory relationship to Muslim identity. Specifically I examine the dialectic between women's narratives and the political space in which the women are situated in Canada. Such a venture helps me complicate the polarizing influences on their lives and identify a hybridized third space, where translation and interpretation determine how lives are lived and narratives are told and retold.[1]

Let me begin with the premise that the politics of being positioned as and/or being responded to as a Muslim place women in a dilemma. In order to demand that issues such as lack of education, violence, poverty, and employment opportunities be addressed, they are compelled to enter political space as Muslim. This is a notion not only with tremendous historical resonance but also with current dynamics grounded in relations of political and economic inequality. Within this space they are confronted by regulating discourses of Islam and Orientalism (among others).[2] Although they have different sources with very different agendas, both reduce *Muslim* to a religious category. In addition, members of minority communities in Canada have to negotiate their lives within a context that promotes and legitimizes multicultural policies and practices. At this intersection, women find themselves thrust into predetermined discourses and practices that help shape their agency and determine their strategies of resistance, often to the extent that progressive politics do not appear possible within the category Muslim.

Islam and Orientalism are often posited as polarities reinforcing a particular logic of Muslim women's identity, which places it into structural ambivalence. Within the category "Muslim woman," individual women are caught in the contradictory and complementary nature of these polarities, negotiating the structural ambivalence by going into and coming out of consciousness of it and by manipulating their resistance to it. I would argue that progressive politics cannot emerge from either Islam or Orientalism but in the in-between hybridized third space.

This book draws upon interviews with fourteen women originally from the Middle East, South Asia, East Africa, and Malta who now live in the Toronto area. The women's narratives indicate that in their daily negotiations and translations of the discourses and structures that help determine their lives, expressions of ambivalence become a necessary part of their response to the structured contradictions of Muslim female identity. Some women name the contradictions and some do not. For some women, the structure of these contradictions remains unclear, yet they express uncertainty and doubt about their identities as Muslim women. Even for those women who are able to articulate their Muslim identity, ambivalence continues to be the ground of their ontological condition. They attempt to resolve the ambivalence by articulating its contradictions but remain mired in the structural contradictions of the category "Muslim."

How individual women negotiate the contradictions in their lives suggests a plurality of ways of performing Muslim identity and/or responding to being positioned as Muslim in North America. Their negotiations challenge the regulatory notions of culture and religion as fixed and static: notions discursively constructed within the duality of Islam and Orientalism. As "hybridized" subjects, they initiate new signifiers and symbols of identities that, I would argue, make progressive politics possible. By opening up supplementary discourses in what has been called the third space, women rescript notions of the original, the pure, and the stereotypical. They resist, contest, and collude through individual and collaborative strategies in the process of cultural, political, and economic empowerment. Their responses to the proposal to have *Shari'a* (Islamic religious law) in Canada provide an example. *Shari'a* is seen by many as central to a Muslim life. Women who continue to support the view that Islam and *Shari'a* are egalitarian nevertheless remain aware of the sexism embedded in *Shari'a*.[3]

Current configurations of Muslim female identity as intrinsic to the construction of "Muslim" are important to the way in which this notion is articulated in cultural relations within the spaces and boundaries of these women's lives. The signification of Muslim women's identity, although drawn from the social, political, and historical context in which they live, also contributes to their condition of existence and negotiation. The women's negotiations destabilize assumptions about the "Muslim woman," serving as examples of the dynamic nature of Islamic female identity. Their narratives help us understand the issues that they and others might face in present-day Western metropolitan societies and suggest how Islamic female identity is constructed and performed in Canada and how it may be constructed and performed elsewhere in the "First World."

As a Muslim feminist academic, I am particularly aware of the constantly shifting ground from which I negotiate my life and from which I speak. While I do not necessarily practice religion, I am nonetheless implicated in and influenced by religious discourse. As such, I face intersecting scrutiny from the colonial, Orientalist, religious, multiculturalist, academic, and feminist gaze. These often dissimilar pressures come from more than just attitudes about Islam and the Muslim. As David T. Goldberg (1990) and J. F. Lyotard (1984) have pointed out, these beliefs are also rooted in the linguistic narratives that help structure our thoughts. Cultural/religious narratives are frequently founded on misleading notions of racial and ethnic purity that deny constantly produced and performed hybridity. They channel us toward binary positions of victims/victimizers and oppressors/oppressed, positions that have explanatory power and are easily recognized as symbols of the "correct" truth. Not only are these divisions dead ends, but the rich complexities of life cannot be contained in their respective homogenized "truths" either.

Although my life does not fit into these essentialist categories, I am constantly pressured to identify "my" single truth. (The pressures differ according to the location that I am in.) As I express my desire for flexibility and the right to be contradictory and confused, which more fully reflects the hybrid nature of my life, I receive subtle and sometimes not so subtle messages that I do not quite fit. My refusal to be slotted into a correct truth results in comments like, "You are not a real Muslim, you are different, you are not like the others." As an Other of the Other in Canada, I am constantly positioned to defend an identity I may not have defended in my "home" country, Pakistan.

While I struggle with issues of identity in my examination of the construct of "Muslim woman" and how particular women negotiate their identities in relation to the concept, I am aware that no single racial, ethnic, or religious group is "the Muslim." Muslim women living in North American diasporic communities come from geographical regions as diverse as China, Iran, and Nigeria. Any attempt to capture their richly diverse cultural and religious expressions would have to face charges of reductionism. I am also aware that my use of the category "Muslim" opens me to charges of reinforcing essentialist notions of originality and authenticism, the very ideas I want to move away from. Let me say then that my use of the term *Muslim* is similar to Chandra Mohanty's (1991a) use of the term "Third World woman." Mohanty draws upon Benedict Anderson's (1983) notion of "imagined community" to speak of the Third World woman as an analytical and political category useful in counter-hegemonic struggle. Also, I draw upon Gayatri Spivak's (1990) notion of strategic "essentialism" in situating my vision of the Muslim woman as part of a strategy to identify and engage with regional, situation-specific, and global struggles. The vision includes religious as well as nonreligious resistance.

This study, then, offers a notion of Muslim women's differences not as a static definitive answer but rather as an opportunity for dialogue and conversation.[4] I accept the category Muslim as a starting point, and through this discussion and my other writings problematize it in an attempt to understand the fluidity of cultural expressions, particularly those within diasporic communities. This investigation is also partly fueled by my own desire to identify and engage with this space of displacement so I can practice feminist politics within the category Muslim. The subjectivities of the women of whom I speak are mediated through their unique national and geographical histories as well as their racial and class locations in North America. I use the term *Muslim* because it serves as a convenient signifier not only to examine stereotypes but to explore how the stereotypes intersect with the self-articulation of migrant diasporic communities as well. Thus, my use of the term *Muslim woman* arises out of these women's postcolonial migrant experience.

Muslim also has a common-sense relevancy. Muslim women in particular are seen in simplistic and limiting ways as part of the undifferentiated group, Muslim woman. They can only be members of religious communities and not thoughtful, independent individuals; and certainly not progressive or feminist. As one of my students said, "Until I took your class, I never, ever thought there was such a thing as a Muslim feminist." Indeed, remarks my students have made at the various universities where I have taught in Canada suggest that they have more or less accepted the Orientalist view of Muslim woman as totally oppressed by religion. Their comments reveal oppositional notions of progressivism and fundamentalism, containing irresolvable differences that could not be "educated" away. Their knowledge base appears to draw upon discourses as diverse as Orientalist, religious, and liberal feminist, as well as popular, culture. Codes and signifiers present in these discourses and practices are accepted as "natural." In particular the veil elicits strong emotional reactions and appears to function as the ultimate symbol of Muslim women's oppression, silencing any veiled women who may be present in the room. Readings and discussions in courses that I have organized have often disrupted this "common sense." We connect material from the unspoken and under-represented colonial past that informs and haunts the students' postcolonial present. We explore the construction of the Muslim and the part it plays in continuing to structure relations of inequality between Euro-America and Muslim communities—not only "Third World" societies, but also diasporic communities within the "First World," where many Muslims live. We examine the rise of fundamentalism and connect it to globalization and growing international relations of inequality. In particular, we consider how the students, their peers and families often have been inadvertently implicated in reinforcing these images. Through engaging with feminist analytical material, poetry, and stories of women's lives, we have been able to disrupt the constant and consistent signification of Muslim women as Other and recognize the hybridity of their lives in North America.

These examples demonstrate the need to rethink how Muslims are positioned and live in a pluralist society. In this discussion, I want to continue these explorations in the "third space," where Homi Bhabha says we can "produce supplementary discourses as sites of resistance and negotiation" (1995, 114). I want to explore the complicated connections between Orientalist understandings of the Muslim Other and community conservatism as they intersect in a space legitimized by multicultural policy and practices. I want to examine this seemingly unbridgeable duality of Orientalism and Islam that encourages an allegiance to either one or the Other and thus discourages the in-between gray zones from which progressive politics often emerges. I want to complicate the term *Muslim* and write in the history that constructs and reinforces the duality of Orientalism and Islam. And I want to challenge liberal feminist calls to free Third World women, in particular Muslim women, from their communities.

Fixed notions of identity informed by Orientalism and Islam are often associated with multiculturalism. These connections strengthen conservative notions of identity politics, thereby not only giving greater authority and legitimacy to patriarchal visions of community but also strengthening stereotypes about the community as well. At the same time, the diversity of the community, and in particular the diversity of feminist positions within that community, is denied as irrelevant. Deliberations that move away from notions of fixity open up the third space, allowing a rescripting with social and political implications. That space enables me to explore the particular ways in which women can struggle against sexism within their families and communities as they challenge, collaborate with, and negotiate the "Third World" spaces allocated to minorities in North America. Such negotiations also help create the space from which Muslim women can reaffirm solidarity with progressive or revolutionary movements back "home" without feeding into racist stereotypes about minorities in North America.

In engaging the topic Muslim women as a field of study, I do not propose to define the struggle of all Muslim women or what form these struggles should take. Neither do I aim to assume an authoritative or a definitive position on Muslim women. Rather, I use stories of gender and sexual identities to help complicate conventional accounts of Muslim women's lives. Through identifying personal issues and personal rites of passage of women living in diasporic communities, I want to identify and assist ongoing struggles of negotiation and translation. My purpose is to open new fields of exploration, to identify for debate that which has been very often neglected, and to challenge that which is taken for granted.

Acknowledgments

This manuscript has benefited from conversations with and input from Roger Simon, George Dei, Angela Miles, Rory Crath, Kathleen Rockhill, Ilan Kapoor, Handel Wright, Jack Brown, Nuzhat Amin, Amina Jamal, Guida Man, Patience Idemudia, Kathleen Moore, Aida Graff, Uzair Qureshi, and Madan Handa. I would also like to acknowledge the patience and support of my children Zainab and Raza.

1

Negotiating the Third Space

Conventional definitions situate ethnic identity as ascriptive (Barth 1969), as a designation that allows for social and political mobilization (Keating 1993), as affiliation or attachment with like-minded people (Fleras and Elliott 1996), or as attributes typical of certain groups and useful in distinguishing communities from each other (Glazer and Moynihan 1975). Such views present us with ideas about ethnicity that focus on aggregates of people who share common static classifiable and unchanging characteristics and who are distinct from each other. Critical features of ethnic groups, Fredrik Barth (1969) argues, include self-ascription and ascription by others (13). Barth, however, does concede that boundaries between ethnic groups are permeable and shifting.

Social theorists working within a cultural studies framework have not only reinforced these notions of permeable and shifting ethnic boundaries but also suggested that ethnicity itself is ever changing. Homi Bhabha (1994c), Gloria Anzaldua (1987), Gayatri Spivak (1993), Trinh Minh-Ha (1989), Paul Gilroy (1992), Stuart Hall (1996), and R. Radhakrishnan (1996), among others, have argued for understanding and expressions of ethnicity that move away from notions of static, authentic, and original culture and identity. Rather, they claim that individuals' daily interactions illustrate their cultural expressions. In particular, Bhabha's notion of hybridized subjectivity in the third space and Gloria Anzaldua's identification of a "mestiza" consciousness become useful tools in helping to understand how individuals negotiate the contradictory demands and polarities of their lives.

By disrupting the concept of original and homogenous culture, Bhabha's (1990b, 1995) notion of third space unsettles a pattern of meaning in serial time and challenges the articulation of culture as a homogenizing, unifying force, authenticated by the originary past and kept alive in the national tradition of the people.[1] Instead, Bhabha points out that individuals construct their cultures from national as well as religious texts and transform them, often into Western forms of symbols, signifiers of technology, language, and dress. These new forms of articulation through a third space transform "the meanings of colonial inheritance into the liberatory signs of a free people of the future"(1994c, 38). In Bhabha's terms, the third space becomes a space of contradiction, repetition, ambiguity, and disavowal of colonial authority (1990b). The dynamic of the third space does not allow for original signifiers and symbols in oppositional polarities. Instead, these same signs are appropriated, translated, rehistoricized, and reread. Such discursive conditions of enunciation allow for possibilities of supplementary sites of resistance and negotiation. "And once it [third space] opens up, we are in a different space, we are making different presumptions and mobilizing emergent, unanticipated forms of historical agency" (1995, 114).

These dynamic and contradictory forms of agency draw upon Bhabha's notion of hybridized states, where dialectic polarities demand the subject's allegiance at the same moment. Hybridized individuals, caught in the discontinuous time of translation and negotiation, erasing any claims for inherent cultural purity, inhabit the rim of an "in-between reality" marked by shifting psychic, cultural, and territorial boundaries. Minh-Ha speaks of this translation as well in "Grandma's Story" when she tells us, "Each woman, like each people, has her own way of unrolling the ties that bind" (1989, 148).

Gloria Anzaldua (1987) is also critical of the categories or bordered spaces where subjectivity is assumed to be enclosed. Women specifically, she argues, are not only alienated from the dominant culture but because of sexism in their communities are also not full subjects in the "mother culture." "Petrified she can't respond, her face caught between *los intersticios*, the spaces between the different worlds she inhabits" (20).

Out of these articulations of compartmentalizations and dualistic thinking, an "'alien' consciousness is presently in the making—a new mestiza consciousness, *una consiencia de mujer*. It is a consciousness of the Borderlands" (77). In mestiza consciousness we are presented with a subject who acts from the confluence of simultaneous oppressive categories. She is the ambiguous, borders-dwelling self whose polarities are turned into strengths, and her subjectivity is never fixed but always in the making. It is through notions of mestiza consciousness, and in particular third space, that I turn to the next section, which helps set the context of Muslim women's negotiations in North America.

Situating Third Space

In his essay "Signs Taken for Wonders" Bhabha speaks to the idea of trans-parency as "the action of the distribution and arrangement of differential spaces, positions, knowledges in relation to each other, relative to a dis-criminatory, not inherent, sense of order" (1994d, 109). Through this imaginative arrangement the subject is neither simply captured in a real-ist narrative nor interpellated through ideology. Bhabha's transparency suggests a creative rethinking and repositioning of earlier and current codes of authority—so much so that the power of recent codes of author-ity (postcolonial, capitalist, nationalist, and religious, among others) can-not be read without being influenced by earlier ones. The effect of these overlapping transparencies, including postcolonial codes of power, is part of the enunciative process that defines the subordinate colonial. The notion of "Muslim woman" is one such subordinate colonial.

The photographic negative image is also part of Bhabha's notion of transparency. Through this reversed image, the Muslim woman as subject is always being constructed in negativity and disavowal.[2] Disavowal in-tensifies the power of colonial and now postcolonial intervention and re-scription in the notion of woman as Muslim. Women's negotiations and translations are coded onto discursive transparencies informed by Orien-talist and Islamic discourse, and these transparencies are over-written in multicultural contexts. Multicultural policies and practices, in a sense, become another transparency. My use of the terms Orientalism and Islam is not intended to set up a monolithic binary. Instead, my aim is to identify hegemonic discourses that are constantly being set up and displaced by the women's narratives. In turning away from the discourse and images of self as the stereotyped Muslim woman, individual women turn toward either the colonizer/West or Islam for affirmation. Instead of affirmation, however, they find devaluations and apprehension in the former (Orien-talism) and mechanisms for their control in the latter (Islamism).

Orientalism

Orientalism draws on stereotypes, which, as Bhabha (1994c) reminds us, are the "fixed and static construction[s] of other as the subject of colonial discourse" (70). Implying disorder and inferiority, the stereotype contains what is already known and must constantly be repeated, thus producing the "colonized as a social reality which is at once an 'other' and entirely knowable and visible" (70–71). This social reality is more than a false im-age: it includes "projection and interjection, metaphoric and metonymic strategies, displacement, over-determination, guilt, aggressivity; the masking and splitting of 'official' and phantasmatic knowledges to construct the positionalities and oppositionalities of racist discourse" (Bhabha 1994c, 81–82).

Edward Said has identified these strategies of colonial power in his classic text *Orientalism* (1979). Said argues that the ideology embedded in Orientalism was shaped by Europe's historical envy, fear, and hatred of the "infidel" and supplemented by its sense of superiority over Islamic societies. Even those who romanticized and valued the Orient were part of this "othering" and homogenizing.[3] Although not all the work of European scholars and writers on Islam is easily dismissible, it was the European ethnocentric accounts that captured popular imagination.[4]

As we move towards the twenty-first century, Orientalist fantasies remain. In particular, societies where Islam is the religion of the majority continue to be seen as totalizing religious and ideological orders. Authors writing within this framework give Islamic religious ideology a pre-eminent position in the Islamic world, while ignoring regional, cultural, and neocolonial differences (Kandiyoti 1991; Moghadam 1991). Thus, religion, which is seen in "normal" societies as one of many institutions, is seen in Islamic societies as the overriding influence, feeding Orientalist assumptions about the role of religion in the lives of individual women.

Orientalist perceptions fueled the determination that the European colonizer did not venture forth as an exploiter. Rather, "he" went out to enlighten and, in the case of the "Islamic world," to deliver women from religious oppression (I will speak to this later in this chapter). While much of Orientalist discourse focused on liberation of Muslim women from Islam, there was also an aspect of Orientalist/colonialist discourse that pointed to the sexual availability of Muslim women. Rana Kabani (1986) argues that the Orient was seen largely as an illicit space and its women convenient chattel who offered sexual gratification denied in Victorian homes. Similarly, Malek Alloula's (1986) collection of commentary and postcards from the time of colonial rule exposes French obsession with the body of the colonial Algerian woman. Not only are the postcards of nude and semi-clad women symbolic of the violence such unveiling would visit on the culture and dignity of the colonized, but they also identify the unequal power relations between women and men as well as colonizer and colonized. Princess Jasmine in the 1994 feature film *Aladdin* provides an example of the eroticized and available Muslim woman of Western popular culture. Moreover, since the 1979 revolution in Iran and the hostage-taking of Americans in Tehran, erotic images have been supplemented by the Muslim woman as the shrouded "terrorist" supporting Ayatullah Khomeini. The potency of these dichotomous images of eroticism and violence is backed by colonialism in its newer form, a combination of economic, political, and cultural imperialism.

Representations of Muslim as Other affected as well as constructed the social and political context in North America in which the Gulf War was waged in 1991, indicating an increase in Orientalist influence and, in particular, its ability to prejudice and reinforce political and military decisions. Zuhair Kashmeri's (1991) documentation of the harassment of Arabs and Muslims in Canada during the war speaks to the ease with which popular prejudice was able not only to influence public policy but also to disrupt the everyday interactions of many Arab and Muslim school children. Prejudice influenced by the popular press and the rhetoric of war emphasized images of overly religious, irrational, barbaric, and fundamentalist Muslims.

Although dominated by masculinist, patriarchal, and Western codes, Orientalism is not a monolithic discourse. Some Orientalists have been feminists, while others are non-Western. As Mohanty (1991b) has pointed out, often Western feminist discursive constructions of the "Third World woman" depict the lives of Muslim women as entirely determined by Islamic ideology and uninfluenced by global socioeconomic and political relations. Mohanty states that her critique pertains not only to Western feminists but also to analysis of "third world scholars writing about their own cultures, which employ identical analytic strategies" (1991b, 52).

Orientalism can also be linked to nationalism. In another context, Pratha Chatterjee (1986) has explored these links.[5] Nationalism, he claims, is strongly influenced by colonial thought. And Margot Badran's (1995) work on upper- and middle-class women connects nationalism to early feminist organizing in Egypt. She argues that feminist consciousness at the turn of the century emerged with the modern nation of Egypt. Chatterjee's and Badran's analyses suggest a link among Orientalism, nationalism, and feminism. Julie Stephens (1989) is also critical of feminist scholarship that claims to speak for "real women" rather than the mythic and idealized woman of nationalist discourse. Stephens claims that feminism often collides as well as colludes with Orientalist discourse in a search for the sovereign female subject and in attempts to represent her. Feminist writings grant subject status to those women who fulfill criteria consistent with the feminist position of the author and, in so doing, valorize some subjects of feminist research while seeing others as objectified and oppressed. Thus feminist analysis also frequently reproduces Orientalist knowledge.

Islamism

Orientalist vision of Muslim women comes from Western scholars (including Third World scholars working within the Western academy), Western media, and the Western popular culture. Although important and valid, the complexities of lives in Muslim societies and communities cannot be reduced to Orientalism. Muslim women's negotiations of their subjectivities are also to a large extent shaped by discourses that draw upon the sacred to legitimize their authority. The sacred books of Islam, like other texts, are interpreted and lived in particular historical, geographical, and temporal contexts, giving rise to Islamic traditions as varied and contested as there are Muslim communities that live them. Yet how do the many geographically and culturally diverse Islams help constitute women's lives, and what role does fundamentalism play in all of this?

Bruce Lawrence (1987) argues that fundamentalism is not a term that Muslims use to describe themselves. And Gita Sahgal and Nira Yuval Davis (1992) make an important distinction between the term *fundamentalist* as an inherent part of the Orientalist description of Muslims and those reactionary movements, often referred to as Islamist, which use essentialist interpretations of Islam to impose their own political agenda. But there is another distinction as well that I think is important for our discussion: modernism. Similarities as well as differences between all of these distinctions must be put in the context of European colonization of Muslim societies and a history that contains not only political defeat but also a submission to European cultural imperialism (Said 1994). Basam Tibi points out: "Modern Islam is a defensive culture. The combination of the European colonial penetration, the decay of the Ottoman empire, and the extension of the technologically more advanced European culture all over the world is seen by the Islamic peoples as signifying a real threat" (1987, 64–65). And it is within this defensive paradigm that we need to understand modern Islam, both modernist and Islamist.

Modernist interpretations of Islam are found in the writings of the turn-of-the-century elite Muslim men from Turkey, Egypt, Iran, Afghanistan, and colonial India, among other places. The writers included Mohammad Abduh, Jamal-u-din-Afghani, Sir Sayed Ahmed Khan, Mohammad Iqbal, and Kamal Ataturk. These men promoted reform in Muslim societies that would modernize their nations and put them in the trajectory of Western-style progress. In particular, they advocated a return to the use of *ijtehad* (analytical reasoning) as a method of instituting change within civil and political institutions in Muslim societies. Modernists argued that *ijtehad* had been used in the past in pre-colonial Muslim societies and could be used again so that reform would proceed within an Islamic frame. A major problem with modernist vision of reform was its dismissal of the structural effects of colonialism not only during colonization but also long after the former colonies had achieved political independence. Although modernists were concerned with getting their message across to the people whose conditions their reforms were to affect, they were also interested in challenging the arguments of European Orientalists and in reaching European readers (Davis 1987). Many modernist writers wrote in European languages and published in European countries. Frequently, these elite men did not enjoy popular support in their own countries but were nevertheless able to influence their governments, and people of their own class generally benefited from the effects of reforms they advocated. In the case of Iran and Turkey, modernist reforms included prohibitions against the veil (Hoodfar 1993) and in the case of Afghanistan legislation against bride price and child marriage (Khan manuscript).

Although both modernism and Islamism promote views of a homogenizing collective, modernism does not question the nation state. Islamist thought, in contrast, considers the national division to be a colonial imposition that must be discarded. Isma'il Raji al Faruqi stresses the importance of a single Islamic society, "a universal Pax Islamica, an Islamic organization institutionalizing and implementing the divine precepts" (1987, 231). A vision of a single society gets situated in binary opposition to the West and capitalist culture, and the view enjoys popular support in many Muslim societies. Solidarity in a single society, within which Islam "intends to remain faithful to its traditions, so as to convey its message and values"(Al Faruqi 1987, 223), proves an enticing message for those excluded from sharing the benefits of capitalism in Muslim societies.

These values include the indisputable determination that *Shari'a* is divine and central to civil and political life in Muslim society (Al Faruqi 1987, 231). Such a society would provide "an alternative to challenges of modern times" (Chatty 1987, 217). Islamist activists oppose social change as un-Islamic. Not only are Islamists critical of modernist reform, but they also view Islamic theological views on reform with suspicion. As Cherif Bassiouni points out, they seek a return to what they perceive as Islamic fundamentals and "advance simplistic views as panaceas for complex problems" (1987, 252). Yet how would a return to an Islamic past pay the debts owed by many Muslim countries? And how would the Muslim past tackle issues raised by globalization of markets?

Islamist movements arose in conjunction with failure of leaders, both secular and religious, to respond to challenges posed by colonization and industrialization. Political Islam became, Detlev Khalid (1987) argues, a method of coping with the challenges of modernity. Through attempts to reduce the complexities of Islamic societies to a totalizing and reductionist vision of Islam, Islamism also promotes a type of Orientalism. Yet Islamism is also a challenge to Orientalism and aspires to rival "foreign" ideologies such as colonialism, communism, and liberalism by seeking the true message of Islam in primary sources, for example, the *Qur'an* and the *hadith* (literature based on Mohammad's teachings). Khalid sees an identity crisis among Muslims as part of the reason for Islamism: "Yet, for Muslims this pride in the 'pristine' simplicity as in the finality and all comprehensive of the Islamist message has been fostered by many of the writings of European Orientalists. A number of their [the Orientalists'] contentions are all too eagerly pounced on by Muslim fundamentalists. While they sincerely believe that they are propagating nothing but the pure Islam of the days of the Prophet and his first 'rightly guided' Caliphs, their teachings are in reality conditioned to a fair extent by the challenges of their assumed adversary, Western civilization" (1982, 130).

Khalid's comments draw upon the Islam-versus-West binary and position Islamism as anti-West and anticolonial. Many activists within Islamist movements recognize that the challenges facing Muslim societies are unfamiliar and, as such, they oppose modernist as well as traditionalist articulations of those challenges. As Bruce Lawrence (1987) points out, Islamism often includes dissident movements against both foreign power and foreign ideas promoted by indigenous elites.

Barbara Stowasser (1987) contends that a return to the basic texts of *Qur'an* and *hadith* is problematic. Particularly the *hadith* contains varied and "often contradictory views on the society that it describes" (264), making it a flexible mechanism through which patriarchal and often despotic interests have been able to create the social orders in many Muslim societies by focusing on restrictive aspects. Women's voices and other voices of dissent have been crushed on the basis of an assumption regarding finality of the divine Islamic message when, in effect, the finality has been contrived to legitimate dominant patriarchal interests.

Although male-dominated, and frequently antifemale, Islamist movements also count female activists among their membership. The political work and writings of Islamist Egyptians Zainab al-Ghazali, founder of the Society of Muslim Sisters, and Safinaz Kazim challenge determinations of what is considered feminist activism. The work of both women reveals an unqualified desire to promote and secure women's empowerment, but criticizes feminism as a Western influence. Yet by the 1980s, as Badran (1995) points out, feminists as well as many women within Islamist movements in Egypt began to articulate similar positions on gender issues, particularly those focused on employment.

Shahrzad Mojab (1995) is not convinced that what has been referred to as "Islamist feminism" is capable of improving women's status in Muslim societies. Referring to the Islamic Republic of Iran, Mojab points out that Islamic feminists want to improve female and male relations within theocratic/political institutions that do not have a history of gender and class egalitarianism. "One can argue," Mojab claims, "that this 'feminism,' far from being an alternative, is a compromise with patriarchy" (1995). Yet in her autobiographical novel, Sara Suleri (1987) questions feminist articulations of woman, which, she says, are not able to formulate the agency of women such as her grandmother. Suleri questions the practice of basing a political movement on the notion of "woman." Instead, she believes that women's subjectivities are constituted through their performance of social roles.

Feminism

The role of feminism in Muslin society needs to be placed in a colonial context. Algeria provides an example. In his influential essay "Algeria Unveiled" Frantz Fanon (1965) persuasively argues that the French were concerned with liberating Algerian Muslim women as a means of gaining control over Algerian men and subordinating Algerian society to French colonialism. The Algerian woman was described as "humiliated, sequestered, cloistered . . . [while] the behavior of the Algerian man was firmly denounced and described as medieval and barbaric" (38). The most symbolic aspect of the humiliation of Algerian as well as other Muslim women continues to be the veil. As Leila Ahmed puts it: "Veiling—to Western eyes, the most visible marker of the differentness and inferiority of Islamic societies—became the symbol now of both the oppression of women (or, in the language of the day, Islam's degradation of women) and the backwardness of Islam, and it became the open target of colonial attack and the spearhead of the assault on Muslim societies" (1992, 152).

Accordingly, a spectacle was arranged in colonial Algeria. Under strict orders from their colonial masters, maids and other poor women were deveiled and paraded. "Every veil that fell, every body that became liberated from the traditional embrace of the haik, every face that offered itself to the bold and impatient glance of the occupier was a negative expression that Algeria was beginning to deny herself and was accepting the rape of the colonizer. Algerian society with every abandoned veil seemed to express its willingness to attend the master's school and to decide to change its habits under the occupier's direction and patronage" (Fanon 1965, 42).

The message in British colonies was similar. All the while British Victorian society was finding ways to contest and dismiss suffragettes and feminists, British colonial authorities were using feminist ideas in the service of colonialism. Other men oppressed their women; therefore, other men are barbaric and not fit to rule the societies in which they live. The activities of Eugene Cromer, British counsel general in Egypt in the late nineteenth century, provide an example. Lord Cromer was particularly interested in the emancipation of Egyptian women, and he believed that the "fatal obstacle" in this emancipation was Islam. Certainly Lord Cromer was not particularly interested in the emancipation of British women, as he was also the president of the Men's League for Opposing Women's Suffrage (Ahmed 1992).

Ideas of liberating colonial women from colonial men were not limited to European men. The idea of empire was also central to concerns of European feminists. Along with the right to vote, suffragettes claimed their rights as citizens of European empires. Serving in the colonies provided them with opportunities not available to women at home. As teachers, missionaries, anthropologists, travel writers, and wives of colonial administrators, European feminists, too, advanced maternal and imperialist notions toward colonial women with whom they came into contact (Strobel and Chaudhuri 1992). Often European women, too, attempted to liberate colonial women from colonial men, and to some extent this type of thinking is found in liberal feminist theory (Mohanty 1991b). Yet as Ahmed (1992) argues, Western feminists want to challenge and change the social relations that promote male domination in their own communities. They don't want to totally discard their society. Yet often there are assumptions within liberal feminism that Muslim women must do exactly that. They must discard their societies in order to be liberated. What are some of the consequences of these assumptions in Muslim societies? It makes feminism very suspect. Feminism is particularly criticized by Islamists who advocate an anti-West, anticolonial position and who homogenize all feminist positions as liberal feminist. Particularly vulnerable to such criticism is a liberal feminist framework that often divorces gender from the larger social and political context in which it is situated.

Feminism, however, is crucial for exploring how gender, capitalism, and patriarchy position groups as subordinate. Feminism is important for identifying local issues and connecting them to the local, national, and international structures. And feminism is vital for imagining progressive alternatives and collective strategies. Yet I imagine a feminism that does not reiterate liberal frameworks that desire to free women from their communities. Rather, I reinforce feminist analyses that examine and challenge hegemonic international institutions that structure particular communities into relations of privilege and disprivilege. Analysis of social and political dimensions allows for a greater understanding of the context in which religious codes and categories are interpreted. Linking the micro of the women's narratives with the macro, the social context in which the narratives are situated, allows an exploration of women's negotiations, not as fixed constant moments of identity but as instances of uncertain cultural meaning. At this point my examination of discursive and material influences on the third space moves beyond an exploration of how Orientalist, Islamist, and feminist codes and categories construct and affect women's sexuality and agency to the diasporic context in which the women are situated. And it is to this I now turn.

Diasporic Context

I share with other social theorists (Ahmed 1982; Bhabha 1994c; Hall 1996; Spivak 1993) the understanding that colonial history continues to be played out not only outside North America but also within. This history of the colonial "adventure," so traumatic for its victims, has been denied and distorted in the combined knowledges and memory of colonizing Europeans. As North America becomes "home" to diasporic communities, displaced immigrants and permit holders, as well as those silent and unaccounted-for who have no legal status, increasingly demand a social and political presence. Such voices disrupt the holism of Western history as sedimented in "the liberal canon."

In moving away from notions of the originary and cultural relativism often found in religious and Orientalist discourse, notions of hybridity and of third space allow for an investigation of how Muslim women negotiate identity with their families, communities, and in other arenas as a cultural and religious practice. Analysis of social and political dimensions then allows for a greater understanding of the context in which religious texts are interpreted and negotiated. For example, within Muslim societies in the Third World, International Monetary Fund (IMF) restructuring influences not only how the sacred is engaged, but also what political and economic effect Islam has on people's lives. In contrast, among Muslim migrant communities in the Third World, reaction to racism often results in conflation of religion and culture as an identity of resistance. Linking the local and the imperial allows me to examine how tensions get lived. Connecting the micro of the women's narratives with the macro, the social context in which the narratives are situated, suggests women's negotiations are not fixed constant moments of identity but instances of uncertain cultural meaning. That "Migrancy . . . forces a recasting of how the body is grasped, how language works" (Alexander 1996, 1). And subjectivity becomes "an interplay of possibilities where the positionalities are only multiple shifting and constantly in flux" (Lavie and Swedenburg 1996, 3).

What does the disruption of home as a stable signifier mean for a subject in a state of flux? Home, as Avtar Brah (1996, 3) suggests, means the desire to belong to a collectivity, a people. Yet the discourses that construct and influence the identity of "my people" or "my home" are contested definitions. And home not only refers to places of origin but also suggests the discourse of everyday experiences rooted in mundane daily rituals of current locations. Diasporic identity is about settling in and about the conditions in which the group was permitted to enter the host country.

For Muslims "home" is often invoked contradictorily in the form of a floating and rooted signifier, a narrative of the Islamic nation. Being a Muslim woman in regions where the majority of the people are Muslim is related to social, economic, and political conditions as well as to the larger national polity. However, my analysis does not focus on women's negotiations in women's "home" countries. Instead, in this discussion I explore women's translations and negotiations of the third space in minority diasporic communities in the First World, where grounding as a Muslim is significantly different from and more fragile than in the women's "home" countries. And where "the shock of arrival forces us to new knowledge. What the immigrant must work with is what she must invent in order to live. Race, ethnicity, the fluid truths of gender are all cast afresh" (Alexander 1996, 1).

Minority communities, particularly in Britain and Canada, have had to negotiate their spaces in a context where multicultural policies are promoted. In the United States, although there are no official multicultural policies, there are similar implicit assumptions in policies dealing with nonwhite and non-Anglo Americans. Multiculturalism has rich and complex ideological and policy implications and forms the backdrop against which Muslim women's negotiations take place. In moving away from assimilationist paradigms—"become like us as quickly as possible"— multicultural policies continue to be a positive step in the validation of "difference." However, the need to focus on difference reinforces the centrality of an original white Anglo culture.[6] The different is made to exist as that which is different from the norm, the original, masking a symbiotic relationship between the two. Each needs the other, not only to exist but also as its boundary.

Within Britain and North America, Anglo culture is the silent original. Ali Rattansi (1992b) argues that Anglo culture's unquestioned centrality within a multicultural frame allows diverse communities to be acknowledged with a much-needed respect, providing space for members of communities to anchor their identity. This acceptance of difference is valid and crucial. Yet important concerns need to be raised about how this difference is defined and used. First, difference is often defined through what Rattansi calls the "sari, samosas, and steelband syndrome" (1992b, 25), the superficial attributes of culture. The "multiculture" paradigm contains assumptions of static, unchanging, and undifferentiated notions of communities that deny their heterogeneity (Rattansi 1992a). In such a manner, material issues confronting individuals are reduced to one or two symbols of oppression. Similarly, predetermined and pre-established stereotypes of Muslim women denote Islam as the cause of all problems Muslim women face. Muslim women are deemed active promoters of religious ideology or passive recipients of prescriptions of religious texts. The reliance on stereotypes denies the heterogeneous nature of communities and frequently further legitimizes "the community" as homogeneous through state policy and funds. Through this view men are leaders and spokespersons of communities and women merely members. Further, the multicultural paradigm leaves the myriad cultures within it unconnected to social and political history. These notions promote views of culture as homogenous with a collective tradition or a monolithic community—a static system of reference. From here it is easy to "leap" to the next step, educating or legislating away differences and the discrimination that accompanies this differentiation. This pedagogical aspect of culture, Bhabha argues (1994c, 34), focuses on the effect rather than the structure of the problem.

Second, the multicultural difference is used to promote the ahistorical notion of "ethnic culture" through safe encounters with the dominant culture (Corrigan 1987). As such, multiculturalism has been widely criticized as a liberal containment of difference that fails to address the hierarchies of power. Instead, the focus on other cultures highlights their difference from the "norm," the dominant yet silent Anglo culture. Although presented as a "mosaic" of all cultures, multiculturalism often reinforces the distinction between whites and nonwhites by labeling the latter as "multicultural" and different (read inferior). Yet the explicit focus of multicultural "difference" is ethnicity, not race. Moreover, there is little understanding of how Euro-Americans are implicated in continued creation and perpetuation of multicultural differentiation as yet another form of hierarchy.

Although cultural differentiation is officially recognized, Lance Roberts and Rodney Clifton (1992) point out that the Canadian state does not favor and fund a multiculturalism that would allow ethnic groups to institutionally consolidate their ethnic identity as separate from other Canadians. Instead, Roberts and Clifton argue, the state promotes a noninstitutionalized symbolic multiculturalism, which allows the flexibility of having both ethnic group membership without the commitment necessary for institutionalized multiculturalism. Similarly, the British state (Asad 1991), while stereotyping the Muslim minority community as a collective, appears to encourage minority members to participate in British life as individuals. This diversity of cultures does not threaten British identity. The politicization of religious tradition by Muslims does, for it questions loyalty to the nation-state and its totalizing cultural project, the hegemony of ruling-class culture. State preference for symbolic multiculturalism occurs in a context where nonwhites frequently find themselves categorized as minorities devalued and excluded from mainstream life.[7] The negative images of culture and community can lead to a self-negation and devaluation and/or to more rigidly enforced rituals drawing on myths of the past.

Yasmin Ali (1992) has examined instances of enforced and reactive traditionalism in England, which she points out is frequently not self-confident enough to tolerate much deviation from the desired ideal because it is felt that existence of "the community" would be threatened. Such positioning reinforces the patriarchs as community spokespersons and leaders. Ali provides an analysis of Muslim women "managed" by community leaders in northern England, where the Muslim community is often presented as one community, where all live in extended families, where all children respect their elders, and where women live under the unquestioning authority of their religion. Such stereotypical views of "the Islamic community" promoted in conjunction with multicultural policies make it easier to deal with "something unchanging represented by authoritative figures who can be co-opted into the margins" (Ali 1992, 110). A similar situation exists in Canada where, as Roxana Ng (1989) observes, the interests and experiences of immigrant women are often subsumed under those of male "community leaders." Women in Canadian multi-cultural immigrant communities frequently find themselves caught between the politics of ethnicity, sexism within their own communities, and racism from the dominant community.

In making a distinction between tourists and immigrants, Tahire Kocturk (1992) maintains that the latter are more interested in preserving their history. While messages that assimilation is the key to success appeal to the Turkish Muslim immigrants in northwestern Europe whom she describes, they also produce anxiety. Although Kocturk's study indicates that these women lead hybridized lives, their perceptions of themselves often center around myths of nationalism. They either distance themselves from those myths or accept utopian versions of the past in attempts to generate stability within marginalized migrant communities. Islam is a religion, but, as Fatima Mernissi points out, Islam is also "a set of psychological devices about self-empowerment and making oneself at home everywhere around the globe in unfamiliar as well as familiar surroundings" (1987, x).

Ali's (1992) work on Muslim migrant communities in Britain identifies a collusion between unequal partners (the state and patriarchal leaders) to maintain a narrow and static definition of community that severely circumscribes the stage upon which women are permitted to perform as political and social actors. Although the predetermined discourses and relations affect and limit women's agency, Ali points out that women do resist sexism. At the same time they are aware that their resistance could strain or damage their relationships with families and communities, leaving them vulnerable in a society where they face not only sexism but racism as well. Ali argues that "modes of identity through religion must be modified" (121) to release progressive energies. Yet what is the history of Muslims in North America through which we may harness this energy?

Muslims in North America

Arabs are portrayed as newcomers, yet Arab presence in the Americas dates back to the tenth century. Voyages made by Arab sailors may well have inspired Christopher Columbus. A recent Italian display of Columbus's belongings included an Arabic book containing an account of eight sailors from Arab Spain who had landed in the Americas. However, Arab presence in North America, in fact the category Arab itself, is not without contradiction. Conventional accounts conflate Arab and Muslims, although the overwhelming majority of Muslims (approximately eighty percent) are not Arabs. And this conflation along with the notion of "Arab as terrorist" may reinforce mainstream fear of Muslims, the third largest religious group in North America. Complicating this is the attempt by some groups who had previously identified themselves as Arab Americans and who now stress other aspects of identity (perhaps in response to increased anti-Arab and anti-Muslim sentiment). For example, some Lebanese Maronites now stress their Phoenician origin, and some Copts now identify with their Pharaonic roots. Recent statements by the fundamentalist group the Muslim Brotherhood reinforce the notion that only Muslims are Arabs. These complications, as Yvonne Haddad points out, pose a perplexing problem for many "Arab Christians who continue to identify themselves as Arabs" (1994, 65).

Contradictions notwithstanding, many self-representations within various Muslim communities often focus on Islamic traditions, which other North Americans must understand in order to know Muslims better (Waugh and others 1991; Abraham and Abraham 1983). These texts frequently present ethnographic accounts of communities organized around notions of "original and authentic" community group identity preserved and lived within the North American context. While many of these communities identify themselves in nationalist terms, Sameer Abraham (1983) maintains that external forces tend to homogenize these communities into the single Arab-Muslim community. And this "community" is further marginalized by slurs, jokes, and stereotypes reinforced through cartoons, novels, and movies (Abraham 1989; Said 1981; Shaheen 1984) and therefore are not only perpetrated by fringe groups in isolated incidents but are also found at the highest levels of mainstream society (Abraham 1994).

In ethnographic descriptions of various Muslim communities we are presented with idealized norms through which the conduct of females is much more circumscribed than that of males. In these accounts females are frequently required to stay within predetermined parameters, while males are able to transgress them with little or no repercussions. For many young women, particularly professional women, the double standard within their families and communities is difficult to accept (Haddad and Smith 1996). Louise Cainkar's (1991) study of Palestinian-American women in Chicago suggests that they have not necessarily benefited from living in America. On the contrary, the women appear to have lost social and kin networks and social autonomy they may have enjoyed in the countries from which they migrated. In North America they have to contend with family and community fears of "contamination" from mainstream society (132).

Muslims in North America have come from many diverse geographical regions, and some are also recent converts. However, "the Muslim community" is assumed to be a single, monolithic religious immigrant community with few class and race differences (Haddad and Smith 1993). It is assumed that Muslim women must submit to arranged polygamous marriages, wear the veil, and be subservient to their husbands (Bilge and Aswad 1996). There is certainly no understanding of progressive engagement with religion or any appreciation of feminist positions among Muslim women.

In Canada

The struggle for control over representational and social practices through which the Muslim woman is defined in Canada needs to be located in the colonial relations of the British Empire. Although Canada was a colony of the British Empire, it was also a "settler colony" with a higher status in the British Empire than many of the former colonies from where Muslims have emigrated. The imperial hierarchy continues not only to influence the contradictory practices that create the Muslim woman in discourse but also to reinforce her position as an inferior subordinate colonial.

Colonial Orientalist discourse is fashioned in relation to broader social and political contexts. Stereotypes of Muslims, whether Orientalist or Islamist, are to a large extent influenced by the West and the unequal power relations between Euro-American and Muslim societies. These unequal relations have an imperial history and are currently embedded in the neocolonial forms of control of "other" societies (Amin 1989).

In Canada individual Muslim women are first delegated to "communities" of the "Other" and then devalued because they belong to those communities. Notions of a monolithic "community" deny the heterogeneous nature of communities in pluralist societies. Patriarchal, ahistorical, and romanticized views of the "old country" deny the fluidity of identity negotiation within immigrant communities. However, escape from or rejection of such entrenched notions of communities, which have a negative presence in the images of popular culture of mainstream Canadian society, leaves women without a sense of belonging. Nahla Abdo (1993) has studied this marginalization of progressive Middle Eastern women in Canada and in feminist circles in particular. She points out that they are "silenced, ignored and oppressed, not only by structures and institutions, but also by the very social movement whose legitimization is largely derived from its opposition to oppression, namely feminism" (74).

Frequently women's issues are mediated through stereotypes held either by community leaders or those in mainstream society. The Canadian film *Voices of Islam*, funded by the Islamic Foundation, provides an example in its portrayal of only women who wear the *hejab* (veil) as Muslim. Not only does such a selective portrayal ignore the thousands of women in Canada and the millions around the world who do not wear the *hejab*, but it also can be read as a response to the Western fixation on the *hejab* as a symbol of the Muslim woman. The film appears to promote the message that there is an Islamic community in Toronto that people can belong to if they follow the prescribed requirements. Particularly for women the requirements contain messages of chaste and modest behavior within predetermined parameters.

Recent court decisions attest to the legal reinforcement of religion as the primary issue for the stereotypical Muslim community (Khan 1995b; Claridge 1995). In these decisions, rights of individual Muslim women as independent members of Canadian society were largely dismissed as irrelevant.

Similarly, Ali (1992) points to the frequent inability or unwillingness of community leaders in England to confront the issues many Muslims frequently face. Within "the Muslim community," often there is a denial that Muslim women actually have issues. There has been a trend among community leaders in Canada to deny that problems such as teenage pregnancy, violence, alcoholism, drug abuse, health problems such as HIV and AIDS, settlement issues, or issues around identity exist within Muslim homes. Thus concerns that should be dealt with have often been ignored. Nira Yuval-Davis (1997, 122), however, describes a recent phenomenon in Britain that occurred along with state allocation of resources for "women's issues." Various religious and other conservative community organizations that seek to reintegrate women into the family have been competing with feminist agencies for state funds. Although Yuval-Davis is speaking of England, organizations in Canada with similar politics have also suddenly "discovered" that services that deal with violence against women and other social problems, such as AIDS and drug-abuse education, are sources of state monies. It will be interesting to monitor where these trends lead.

Although frequently patriarchal and conservative, community spaces are important, for they tend to replicate and replace the kinship networks many immigrants have left behind. Some male and female members uphold conservative ideals of a religious patriarchal community. Yet for other women, the communities have become prisons. Security in the communities conflicts with opportunities available in the larger society, which appear to offer more rewards and more freedom. If women move toward those perceived freedoms, there is a price to pay. They will face exclusion from their communities as well as discrimination and exclusion from mainstream life. If they stay within their communities, they face increasing control over their mobility and sexuality. These communities are diverse racially and culturally, and yet the heterogeneous and at times contradictory voices get subsumed under the rubric "the Muslim community."

Recent debates on the veil in Canada provide an example. My earlier analysis (Khan 1995c) of the Toronto-based coverage of the debates in Quebec indicates that Muslim feminist voices were not solicited. Instead, media coverage of the surrounding controversy reinforced the us/them binary, oppressed and free, thereby strengthening the Orientalist view of the veil as oppressive and the Islamist view of the veil as liberating. While feminist analysis (Hasan 1992; Hoodfar 1993; Khan 1995c) indicates that the energy surrounding the veil is restless and revisionary as it expands the present into a contradictory site of empowerment, mainstream debates on the *hejab* in Canada illustrate how religion, racism, sexism, and multiculturalism intersect to categorize Muslim minority communities in primarily religious terms while assuming them to be internally homogenous without conflicts. Multiculturalism in Canada works to erase ethnic or national difference so that women who are first- and second-generation and from different countries and racial groups come to occupy the position "Muslim woman."

In order to understand this homogenization and reductionism, Bhabha (1995) proposes an exploration of the construction of cultural difference. He suggests that both the pedagogical (understanding of the signs) and the performative (understanding of the process of signification) be used in passage through a third space, which challenges the notion of culture as a unifying force legitimized by an original mythic and utopian past. Bhabha argues that "all cultural statements and systems of enunciation are constructed in this contradictory and ambivalent space of enunciation" (1995, 37). Fanon (1967) calls this a zone of occult instability where everything is called into question. Here, articulations of new cultural demands, meanings, and strategies in the present become practices of collusion and resistance.

Notwithstanding the references to *Umma* in religious discourse and popular imagination, Dossier III of the international group Women Living under Muslim Laws reminds us: "While similarities exist, the notion of a uniform Muslim world is a misconception imposed on us" (cited in Patel 1991, 95). Increasingly this misconception becomes influential as postcolonial Muslim nations scatter. Bhabha calls this a gathering of the "past in a ritual of revival" (1994c, 139). In diasporic gatherings in North America, ritualized myths of home assume singular importance. Imaginings of the nation, the *Umma*, influence the rituals of identity of diasporic peoples from many nations, even when the performance of the rituals may be different from the cultural roots of the migrants. Although highly idealized, the myth of the *Umma* can provide a social reference in a context where Orientalist stereotypes also other the Muslim colonial subject in discourse. For some, notions of a mythical idealized community along with Muslim identity become an empowering narrative strategy within minority communities. Several of the women whom I interviewed for this study pointed out that they themselves as well as the men in their communities were more interested in following and enforcing religious prescriptions in Canada than they had ever been in their countries of origin. These strategies, although born out of a need to survive, also reinforce the very stereotypes that make survival difficult. Moreover, a need to find security within Muslim minority communities in a context where multicultural policies are promoted tends to reinforce notions of homogenized community receptive to Islamism.

I began this study with a dilemma that Muslim women face. Let me reiterate it here. In positioning themselves to demand changes in lack of education, violence, poverty, and lack of employment opportunities, women have to enter political space as Muslim. Within this space they are connected to the *Umma*. This connection reinforces their central position as woman in the struggles for social, political, and moral order in their "home" countries. Notion of woman is also central in helping define the struggles and boundaries of minority communities in the West. All this is occurring in a context where increasingly Orientalism and Islamist-influenced notions of *Umma* define polarizing influences on women's lives. Thus, issues that women are demanding become the concern of the nation or the community. These issues are then prioritized behind those of achieving a "correct" ideology and morality. "Proper" behavior of women demarcates those who belong to the collective and those who do not, those whose demands will be taken seriously and those who will be dismissed.

Yet what are some of the contradictory and contentious issues for a woman who either codes herself or is coded by others as Muslim? First of all, there is an elision and eclipse of the representations of different Islams.

In North America racialization of Muslim is connected to fundamentalist Islam, and there is little indication of a distinction between Islamic and Islamist in popular imagination. The word Islam frequently suggests a fundamentalist faith-driven politics and evokes images of the "barbaric Muslim Other," while failing to consider the strength of other fundamentalisms such as Christian, Hindu, Jewish, communist, cult dogma, and so forth.

As I argued earlier, views about Islam are also often influenced by populist political Islamist movements. These politicized, frequently anticolonial, anti-West movements exert increasing social and sexual control on the symbolic and chaste woman centered at the core of an identity politics (Moghadam 1991; Helie-Lucas 1994). Islamist religious visions emanate from Muslim religious leaders who are in diasporic communities in the First World as well as those from Muslim societies. Diverse national, regional, social, political, and economic concerns intersect with varied interpretations of sacred texts to produce contradictory views partly in response to the pressures of Western imperialism in its manifold permutations. When women "alienated" by Orientalism turn to Islam for identity, they often face Islamist attempts to contain their bodies within rigid sexist structures.

Islam, and in particular current politicized Islamist views of identity, presents one model for Muslim women in diasporic communities in the First World; Orientalism presents another. In suggesting two poles I do not want to reinforce a binary of Islam and the West. Instead, my aim is to identify discourses that are being constantly articulated not only through the women's narratives but also in their social context. At the same time these discourses are being unsettled, contradicted, and resisted. The social constructedness of the two positions notwithstanding, Orientalism and Islamism are not only split from each other, but are also split within themselves. Orientalism contains racist colonial imagery, but it also affirms the Muslim woman in the dominant discourse (although a negative one) where she would otherwise be absent. Orientalist texts not only affect Westerners but also influence how the colonial subject constitutes herself (Said 1979). Following Bhabha's (1990a) line of argument, an "Orientalist" turning away from the stereotype can be a source of affirmation for the colonial subject as it allows her to disassociate from a devalued Other.

Orientalism and Islamism act as two contradictory poles of desire/ affirmation and aversion/disorientation and help reinforce a structured ambivalence within the notion of the ideal Muslim woman. Both poles essentialize the ideal Muslim woman and reduce her to similar symbols and icons. Algerian feminist Marnia Lazreg (1990) points to the uncanny similarity between "Western" feminist discourse on women from the Middle East and North Africa and that of theologians' own interpretations of women in Islam. The similarities between the construction of knowledge in Orientalist and Islamist discourse indicate how dominant Western stereotypes and Islamist visions of authority intersect. Both reduce the category of Muslim to "the religious," and both encourage debate either within or outside this category. The religious category so constructed is subject to many regulating influences that determine the spaces from which Muslim women are able to speak. At this intersection Muslim women find themselves inserted into predetermined discourses and practices which to some extent shape their agency and determine their strategies of resistance. To an extent, the regulating pressures that I face as a Muslim woman determine the parameters of this discussion.

Although seemingly similar, there are complex differences between reductionism offered by Islamist and Orientalist views that are beyond the scope of this discussion. Suffice it to say that Orientalists offer descriptive and devalued essentialist imagery of Islam as articles of faith.[8] Islamists, however, address women's contemporary needs by presenting Islamically inspired solutions enforced through persuasion and, at times, coercion (Moghadam 1991; Stowasser 1987). Orientalist and Islamist narratives pose a dialectic that appears irresolvable; their differences cannot be persuaded or educated away.

The women's narratives that are portrayed in the following chapters do not disavow, resolve, or transcend the contradictions between Orientalism and Islam. Instead, in their daily negotiations, the women open up a supplementary space, where as hybridized subjects they translate the polarities of Orientalism and Islam into the politics of race, ethnicity, migrant communities in the diaspora, and family life. Moreover, the image of the Muslim woman in Canada, which is at once familiar yet not quite "doable," often produces emotional responses to the contradictions that the women face. Some women name, resist, and challenge the contradictions and express this emotional uncertainty. Other narratives suggest that the women resist through their refusal to accept in their daily life Orientalist and Islamist codes, categorizations, and prescriptions for behavior. However, all the narratives indicate differing degrees of doubt and disorientation. Regardless of whether they express uncertainty, all the women's narratives are constrained within the structured ambivalence of the construct Muslim woman, so much so that, even if some women disavow Orientalist colonial stereotypes and Islam, they cannot escape the structural bind within which the construct places them.[9]

However, the multiple determinations and uneven discourses deployed to signify the Muslim woman do not define reality for actual Muslim women in Canada. Their lives, although affected by colonial/racist stereotyping and religious ideology and prescriptions, are also affected by the regional and geographical issues of their countries of origin. For each of the women interviewed, being a Muslim meant a different reality, both in terms of their understanding of Islam and in the daily practices of their lives. Although discursive determinations of Muslim femaleness do not describe their day-to-day reality, individual Muslim women inevitably confront predetermined codes and signifiers and the contradictions contained within them. These women must face not only ambivalent forms of knowledge about themselves but also their own ambivalent responses to that knowledge.

Subjects of Study

I interviewed sixteen Muslim women for this research. My criteria included women who had been born into Muslim families as well as those who identified themselves as Muslim. Although originally from different countries, they all currently live in the Toronto area.

To find my subjects, I asked friends, colleagues, and women's groups to ask suitable individuals to contact me if they were willing to talk about what their experiences of being Muslim and female in Canada mean. I suspect that those who referred these women to me had discussed with the nominees something about Muslim identity and whether they wanted to raise questions about the issue or just talk about it. So the commonalities that are evident among the women are not necessarily incidental. To some degree, they are the resut of a chain reaction in which I asked one person to recommend another who wanted to talk about Muslim identity. Karima is the only woman whom I did not find through this type of sampling. As part of the interview process, Safieh and I had gone out for lunch, and Karima was our waitress. She said that she was a Muslim from Iran, and I asked her if she would be willing to be interviewed about her experiences in Canada.

I had originally envisioned an empirical approach and used a questionnaire that posed questions about age, education, and employment experiences (see appendix). As the interviews progressed, I began to see patterns in the women's responses, which led me to devise an interview format more like a conversation. I found this less structured approach more useful in helping to unfold and identify the contradictions that women displayed.

Although sixteen women were interviewed, I have chosen to eliminate the presentation of material of two women from this study. The issues they raised were thematically repetitive to those of the women whose interviews I do present. This elimination makes the presentation of the argument of the thesis more succinct.

The women I talked with are mainly middle class, and in part this commonality is influenced by the point system that governs immigration to Canada. This system is highly selective, and very few, if any, rural and urban poor people immigrate to Canada. Even those women whose class position in Canada is working class normally come from somewhat affluent backgrounds in their countries of origin. For example, on the surface, Karima appears to be different, as she works as a waitress in Canada while the other women are more middle class. Yet Karima had a middle-class life in Iran, where her husband was a manager.

Three women belonged to Muslim minorities: Musarrat and Iram are Shia;[1] Zubaida is *Ahemedi;*[2] the other thirteen women belong to the Sunni majority.[3] I interviewed the women individually between August 1991 and December 1992. The interviews lasted between one and two hours, and all but one were face to face. I interviewed Iram over the telephone. I also telephoned several women to clarify points. The interviews were held in my office, my home, the university, a school of religious instruction, and two were held in restaurants. During the interviews no one else was present, except in Karima's case, where Safieh acted as her interpreter.

No doubt the women have had new experiences since the study was conducted, but I decided not to contact them for follow-up interviews. This book is not about linear narratives—indeed, to have done such interviews would have reinstated the notion of linearity in women's lives. Instead I want to look at the confluence between the personal and the structural in the conversations of diasporic Muslim women.

To address the issue of generalizability that such a sample raises, I refer to Dorothy Smith's work: "The particular 'case' is not particular in the aspects that are of concern to the inquirer. Indeed, it is not a 'case' for it presents itself to us rather as a point of entry, the locus of an experiencing subject or subjects, into a larger social and economic process" (1987, 157). Although I use Smith's (1987) views to say that representation is not an issue, I need to extend her theorizing to include a certain amount of representativeness. My sample has certain structural constraints vis-à-vis education because of the women's common class location, particularly in their countries of origin. This analysis is also geographically limited to women who are originally from Iran, Pakistan, India, Somalia, Egypt, Turkey, and Malta.

As a Muslim woman invested in exploring Muslim female identity, my research was subjective. My interest in women's narratives led me to an ethnographic collaboration with the interviewees. I was able to negotiate a process through which, as Sandra Kirby and Kate McKenna (1989, 78) suggest, I was able to do research *"with* and *for* participants rather than *on* them" (emphasis theirs). While my primary aim was to let the women speak for themselves, there were also times when I interjected or clarified. The spontaneous discourse and narrative accounts so coproduced reveal daily negotiations in Canada: theirs and to some extent mine as well.

Although I am using the stories of the women as examples, I make no claim to explain the lives of these women. Instead I will draw specific examples from my interviews of how the women who are quite different from each other enact their own relationship with Islam on the one hand, and various sets of social relationships within Orientalist and multiculturalist knowledge production on the other. In so doing, I will identify this interplay and elaboration of what it means to negotiate a Muslim identity in Canada.

The respondents' names have been fictionalized, and their narratives provide examples of how they challenge and resist as well as engage and collaborate with how Muslim identity is constructed in Canada. Their modes of interaction range from disavowal of Islam to researching and selecting for themselves what they will believe. For the purpose of discussion, in each of the following three chapters I have grouped subsets of the fourteen women in terms of the similarity of their personal confrontation and negotiation with Muslim female identity in Canada. The next section of this book deals with women's self-narrations and their intersections with the category Muslim Women as a form of representational North American practice. Do women position themselves in opposition or in conformity with the discourses? Or both?

3

Resolving the Contradictions through Disavowal

The notion of unity ideologically embedded in the concept of Muslim and the differences each woman brings to the narrative in terms of her own desires and social, economic, and cultural location and resources are two aspects of the contradictory position of Muslim women. The interplay between unity and difference is reinforced in Orientalist and Islamist discourses. Such structural positioning, which leads women to experience these contradictions in a way that escapes from the parameters of Muslim woman, seems impossible. And women's narratives suggest ambivalence in their feelings, talk, and behavior, expressing emotional uncertainty and indecision.

In attempts at resolving the ambivalence that the individual women encounter in the construct, some women attempt to reject identification as Muslim women and the uneven determinations that produce contradictions in their lives. It is to these women that I now turn. Safieh, Zubaida, and Nikhat appear to be responding to the race and gender position in which they have been constructed by dominant discourses.

Structural ambivalence appears connected to emotional apprehension and dissonance, aversion from and desire for the categorized image of Muslim. Caught with the emotional dissonance, Safieh, Zubaida, and Nikhat disavow Islam. Yet religion is only one of the multiple discourses deployed in the construction of Muslim female identity. Disavowal of Islam does not mean other discourses that inform and construct Muslim female identity do not impact on their lives. Although they do not identify themselves as Muslim, there are still a range of ways they encounter the construct and enact a Muslim identity. For instance, they are still categorized as belonging to Muslim communities, are viewed through stereotypical assumptions held about Muslim women, and/or find themselves

reacting to being labelled a Muslim woman. These women find that disavowal of themselves as Muslim does not mean that they encounter less
sexism or are able to resolve the exclusionary status in which they are
positioned in Canada. Disavowal of Islam, however, does place them at
odds with their community and families. Hence they end up facing not
only exclusion from the dominant culture but frequently ostracism as
well from their families and communities. Safieh, Zubaida, and Nikhat's
narratives suggest that they want to escape from the contradictions of
being Muslim through disavowal and even conversion to another religion, but cannot. This leads them to expressions of emotional ambivalence, despair, and disorientation.

Safieh

Safieh is twenty-six, white-skinned, and originally from Iran. After she
finished high school in 1983, for two years she tried unsuccessfully to get
admission into the University of Tehran. In 1985 she went to the United
States for further study partly because she could not get admission in a
university in Iran, but also because she and her family believed that a U.S.
degree would have more prestige than a degree from Iran. At the time of
the interview in 1992, she had been in Canada for three and a half years.
Safieh originally intended to return to Iran. Now, although she wants to
visit, she does not think she will ever return to live in Iran. Instead, she
wants her whole family to move out of Iran to Canada or to the United
States because it is not safe for them in Iran. She has lived through the war
with Iraq, and she remembers that two streets away from her house there
had been heavy bombardment. She blames the war on Saddam Hussein
and Ayatullah Khomeini:

> Safieh: Two dictators were sitting there . . . and the people [on both
> sides] are paying for something they didn't do . . . and they are talking
> into the camera, "Yes Saddam is good; yes Saddam is," and I go, "Like,
> how could you be so stupid?" I remember the people back home, that
> we have, too, [said] "Khomeini is great," and I say, "How could you be
> so stupid?" so I am just upset that they don't have the insight into what
> is happening with them.

She thinks that people in Canada put a label on her when they learn that
she is Iranian. It makes her furious that people think most Iranians have
the same ideas as Khomeini.

In a sense Safieh's story is an illustration of the multiple determinations of Muslim female identity in Canada. Her negotiation with Muslim

identity has been significantly influenced not only by growing up in Iran but also by her reaction to sexism in her family in Iran and Canada.

Safieh says she found the Islamic vision of life, as she knew it to be, too narrow, as it could not explain the reason for existence to her. She also found the sexism too hard to live with; consequently she no longer considers herself a Muslim.

> Safieh: Islam couldn't explain to me what was happening in life. It was too narrow, it couldn't explain life's existence. . . . And the sexism bothered me. It is the whole idea of the culture mixed with religion, because forget about covering your hair, I was [asking] them . . . why my cousin which [sic] is a male can go out and have a great time, coming home at 8 o'clock at night, but . . . [I] have to be out with a supervisor, somebody older than me, and I have to be home before sunset?

Safieh could not go out without a chaperone in Iran. Coming to Canada has allowed her more personal mobility and decision-making power. Even before the revolution in Iran that brought Khomeini to power, she recalls, there were two sets of rules, one for boys and one for girls.

> Safieh: From the time that I remember we always have arguments and fights, and I always thought that it wasn't fair that I can't do anything that my brother does. Then when I became seventeen my older brother was gone to the [United] States, and my younger brother [who was four years younger than me] . . . he can go out. . . . For me it was a struggle to get permission to go out. You know what I am saying? They don't want anybody to talk behind your back.
>
> Shahnaz: So you found it restrictive?
>
> Safieh: I found it annoying.
>
> Shahnaz: Did you find it much different in the [United] States?
>
> Safieh: Oh, yes, I remember when I was in New York, I used to rush home before sunset, and I couldn't understand why I was home when the sun was going down. Even when in New York, I start going out at three o'clock in the morning. I wasn't doing anything. I was sitting in a park and reading a book at three o'clock in the morning. I was in a park in a school campus, in front of the security guard's booth. My older brother never asked "Where were you?" [or] "Why you came home so late?"

Safieh's mobility was extremely restricted in Iran, a restriction her parents and brothers enforced. Marie-Amie Helie-Lucas (1994), one of the founding members of the international network Women Living Under Muslim Laws, argues that women as guardians of Islamic identity are potential traitors and need to be watched. Safieh's brother, who used to monitor her mobility in Iran, did not question her in the United States. It could be that in Iran, Safieh's brother felt societal and family pressure to be responsible for the honor of his sisters. He appears to have let go of such a need in the United States.[1]

Safieh has developed an explanation of why control of Muslim women appears necessary:

> Safieh: They [the men] are scared of losing you because the only thing that connects you to them, in their mind, is them being strong, because they don't have anything else to give you. . . . The only thing they can give you is protection. And when you can do everything by yourself, you don't need their protection. . . . Islam helps them, and you don't feel that you need it.
>
> Shahnaz: So in a way, when you reject Islam, you reject this protection?
>
> Safieh: I don't want them to think that I am a little baby they can take care of.

Safieh claimed that the sexism in Islam bothered her. "It is the whole idea of the culture mixed with religion." Partly as a way of rejecting the control Muslim women are subject to, and also because she found herself in the philosophy of Judaism, Safieh decided to convert to Judaism three years ago. She became Jewish, she claims, because Judaism not only inspired her but was also close to her own spiritual state. She found the conversion liberating and now feels closer to God. She says she could have been inspired by Sufis or even Buddhists, yet there were none around. There were only Jewish people around to inspire her. The conversion was probably a response to her existing ambivalence. However, the ambivalence she expressed in the interview is, in fact, one that continues and perhaps is even exacerbated by her conversion. Socially, she is connected to the Iranian community as well as her Iranian Muslim family who do not know of her conversion. She responds to pressures and demands from them. She is particularly concerned about what her mother's reaction would be. Only her brother is aware that she has become Jewish.

> Safieh: I never told my mom; my family don't know it. Only my brother knows it.
>
> Shahnaz: What does your brother say?
>
> Safieh: Well he is Jewish, too, and it is great to have him.
>
> Shahnaz: Why didn't you tell your family about yourself?
>
> Safieh: I didn't tell them, because, oh, God, I don't think they can take it. With my brother they can take it, and he has a big star on his chest and

she [Safieh's mother] knew, she notices . . . she accepted it, but with me she can't. With him he was always different.

Shahnaz: He is a boy, he is allowed?

Safieh: Yes, with me it is different, because I will mother children.

Since Safieh has converted to Judaism, she believes she can be free of the protection/control of her Muslim relatives. She has no Jewish relatives who want to control her. Her brother has given up trying to "protect" her in North America. It isn't clear whether this is because of his own conversion to Judaism or because he is too busy living his own life in the United States. However, for Safieh's mother, it is crucial that her daughter remain Muslim so that she may impart Islamic values to the next generation. Yet Safieh points out, "If I am Jewish, then all the children will be Jewish. Well, I am happy you know." However, Safieh's Jewish children will still be part of the extended Iranian Muslim family. Safieh's husband has not become Jewish, although Safieh says: "I wish he was. . . . He believes in communism."

Safieh continues to feel the effect of control and segregation of women within her extended Iranian family in Canada. She says that her brother-in-law is sexist and "drives her nuts." She complains of the frequent "men's nights out" her husband has with him, from which she is excluded.

Safieh: He [Safieh's brother-in-law] calls up, and he takes my husband out. I like to spend time with my husband because I don't have anybody else. . . . [At family gatherings,] the women have to serve dinner and lunch. They go sit in the other room because they have to gossip about other things. I always like to sit in the room where the men are, because all the discussion and all the good things are happening in that room. . . . With the group of women . . . they always cook . . . talk about cooking. They always talk about their kids. . . . Where the men are talking there was always something happening. It is not proper for me to come [there] because they may say some bad jokes.

Although her in-laws all profess to be communists and do not believe in exploitation, Safieh says that they are sexist and exploitative in their behavior toward their wives and toward her. Safieh's conversion does not resolve the dissonance around segregation. She appears to realize that men's spaces have more power than women's spaces and inserts herself into the men's space.

The contradictions embedded in the construction of Muslim women contain Orientalist notions of liberating women from Islam and devalue the role of patriarchy and sexism in women's lives, particularly in Euro-

American cultures. Safieh believes that by rejecting Islam, she is rejecting the "protection," the control, and the sexism that impact on Muslim women. Yet after having lived in North America for three and a half years, she realizes the extent of sexism in the culture here.

> Safieh: When I see TV, I see in some [ways] it is different, while in some ways it is not. There are two things you can say about what is happening in this society. You could say in one sense that women choose to be what they want to be. If they want to be naked in front of the camera, they have the right to be, and they are going to do it; that is the freedom in this country. In another sense you say that they would be used as a sex object.

In Iran, control of women and the sexualization of women were overt, while in Canada they are in coded language. The practices are different, but the message is the same.

> Safieh: I get confused because in one way I have to be strong. I have to be able to have a career. I have to be, because in this country, if you don't, the woman who sits home and takes care of the children . . . they put her down . . . while in Iran they build her up. I don't like being pushed in either way; I just want to be left alone, so I could be whatever I want to be.

> Shahnaz: So what you are saying is that you are being controlled here, too, in a way?

> Safieh: Yes.

The pressures on Safieh from within her family (as well as those that result from her conversion) and the pressures from a consumeristic society delineate the boundaries within which choices are open for her in Canada. She claims that within her family she is offered "protection," and there is less expectation to succeed in a career. In return she is asked to submit herself to community and family (her in-laws), demands that Safieh finds sexist. Outside the community and family, she has the option of disregarding traditional constraints and seeking gratification within the dominant culture. There she does not face similar limits on her mobility and sexuality. However, she faces other pressures.

> Safieh: As soon as you say you are Iranian, a label is put on you of being from a country which has gone through revolution, which was harmful to other countries. . . . [The taking of] hostages and [the leadership of] Khomeini [helped create this label]. And [they think that] people who let Khomeini's kind be their leader are stupid.

> Shahnaz: How does that make you feel?

> Safieh: It makes me furious that some people could be so stupid that

fifty million people in one country have the same ideas that Khomeini does. . . . And they ask, "How do you like Khomeini?" That is the first question, . . . and I see that these people don't know anything about politics and what happened to my country. They say, "How about Khomeini?" "Oh, you can't go back, can you?" "What do you think about putting this scarf on?" and "Yes, it is better for you to stay here instead of going back there." I know they are right; it is better for me to stay here.

The questions that Safieh alludes to provide evidence of her being stereotyped in the dominant culture. Yet because of the economic and political situation in Iran, as well as the sexism in her family, Safieh is unwillingly placed in the position of agreeing with the statement that it is better for her to stay in Canada. This admission appears a painful contradiction for her.

In Canada, Safieh grants that she has some choice in dealing with the sexism that seeks to control Muslim women. However, she also faces consumerist and achievement pressures:

Safieh: It just makes me feel that, boy, I have so much to do because, I have to do it, in order to be respected. I have to be a mother who has a career outside, and who is productive. You have to have a career, which is good, so you will be respected in your husband's eyes. . . . You can't do it . . . You are human; how can you do everything and always be there for other people when they need you?

Shahnaz: Is anybody there for you?

Safieh: I don't think so. I mean I don't know, maybe my parents. I don't even know if my husband is there for me or not.

Shahnaz: You are not sure?

Safieh: I am not sure.

Shahnaz: Are you there for yourself?

Safieh: No, I don't think so, not for me either, for me, no. [Laughs.] Sometimes I think I have pity on myself, which is not good, because this pity is not a constructive kind of pity.

Shahnaz: What would be a constructive kind of pity?

Safieh: That is another thing, why pity has to be constructive. You know why does everything have to be constructive? Can't you just sit and cry for the sake of crying? . . . But you are not allowed. It is society in general, but it is me, too. I don't allow myself to be human, and what does that mean, being a human? Being alone? Being accepted, even if you make a mistake. I can't accept myself, when I make a mistake, and I always make a mistake [cries].

Safieh feels pushed into consumerism and to be accomplished in Canada. Television is always showing images of the latest product people have to buy. There are also demands on her to be thin, beautiful, and get a university education. She feels that her cousins at home in Iran to some extent have an easier life, as they do not have the same demands put on them. Also, because she is in Canada, her family has expectations of her. She should have "achievements," such as educational credentials to show for her time spent in Canada. However, because of the delay in the sponsorship process, she does not even have her B.A. and can attend university only if she pays the high foreign-student fees. This situation leaves her frustrated and angry at the system and at her husband.

> Safieh: There is too much pressure on you. . . . Everything is being blown up and advertised so big that you have to have it; you can't go without it. You can't go without a beautiful body; you can't go without a Mercedes. I have to work like a horse now, so when I am fifty I can retire. You might be dead when you are working like a horse. . . . My husband he helps me a lot, . . . but I don't think he understands. . . . I don't even like the idea of being in love with somebody. . . . It takes away from my independence. I think it was good talking because I was trying to find out whatever it is that is making me so upset, . . . and I always take [sic] the blame on me; it is me who is doing things wrong. If maybe I look closely and see that other people have the same problems and other women go through this part of life then maybe I will feel better [cries].

The various pressures on Safieh have informed her understanding of who she is and what she wants. She cries because she feels the pressures and is pulled in different directions: from her family to be a Muslim daughter, sister, and mother, sexist pressures from her in-laws, as well as pressures from capitalism to be a consumer. She appears unclear of her priorities. She can't fulfil all the demands because they are contradictory, and she feels depressed and seems to recognize the contradictions that she is a part of. When Safieh begins to name the multiple contradictions that she cannot resolve, her clarity and depression link what she is saying to the next woman in this chapter, Zubaida.

Safieh is a converted Jew facing demands from a Muslim family in a context where she is stereotyped as a Muslim. She is also caught in the structural polarities of Orientalist stereotypes and the control of women promoted by Islamism. She feels an aversion to both and appears disoriented. Changing her religion for Safieh is part of an attempt to resolve the polarizing pressures that she is subjected to and to move into a third, more affirming space. In this space she claims she has no Jewish family prescribing and enforcing Jewish rituals as she has with her Muslim family. Safieh's conversion centers around the spiritual and religious aspect of Muslim female identity. She is still facing other pressures because she is linked to a family and community structure that also help determine and influence her life.

Zubaida

Zubaida is brown-skinned and came to Canada from Pakistan in 1979 when she was twenty-one. It was a family decision. Zubaida had a boyfriend in Pakistan, and she had not wanted to move. They communicated by phoning and writing to each other for three years. He applied and was accepted as an immigrant to Canada but changed his mind at the last minute. He decided not only against immigrating to Canada but against continuing his relationship with Zubaida as well. He did not want to leave Pakistan or his job, and his parents arranged a marriage for him. Zubaida went into depression. She was angry at her parents, their decision to move, and the restrictions on her mobility, and, as I will show, she is angry at being situated as Muslim.

Zubaida does not believe in God and has decided she is no longer Muslim. Yet she is still positioned as a Muslim woman around the issues of dress, control by family, sexuality, and her relationship with her husband, as well as by sexism within the community and at the mosque. These confrontations are exacerbated by her educational experiences, particularly by her discomfort in speaking English, and by the racism she encounters in Canada.

Issues of dress and the speaking of English are informed to an extent by Zubaida's experiences at two very different schools that she attended in Pakistan. The first twelve years of her schooling were at a school where the uniform consisted of *shalwar, kameez,* and a *dupatta,* which was compulsory as a head covering.[2] There were other restrictions. Girls had to cover their heads while playing sports and they were allowed to take part in sports only within the school, not in events off the premises. She recalls that they had to read the *Qur'an* two hours a day:

> Zubaida: And if you have your period, you were exempted from reading the *Qur'an,* and which we used sometimes to our advantage, if we were not prepared for the test. Or if we did not want to, then we would say we can't.

Although Zubaida did not think about it at the time, in retrospect she finds such requirements oppressive.

Zubaida: Having to wear *shalwar kameez* did not make me feel oppressed; it was my dress.

Shahnaz: What was it that made you feel oppressed?

Zubaida: I think it was the whole environment. . . . it took me a lot of years to get over that principal [and the] terrorizing effect that she had.

Shahnaz: Tell me about this terrorizing effect.

Zubaida: The head covering, that was what it came down to. . . . I mean it had to be maintained at all times when you were at school.

Later she was forced to speak in English at the convent school she attended. She found the compulsory head covering more restrictive than speaking English, which she claimed "gave you more status in Pakistan." As Alistair Pennycook (1992) points out, English has become the language of power and prestige in many countries, particularly in professional discourse. However, overvaluation of the colonizer's language can have disastrous effects on the colonial child. Recalling her experiences at the convent school, Zubaida said the emphasis was on English:

Zubaida: Urdu was compulsory, but it was one course. Everything else was in English, and of course the teachers spoke in English, the principal spoke in English, and the whole environment was different, almost a complete opposite to what I had been used to. So I spent [the] first couple of years just sitting and watching people. That is what I thought I could do. I didn't feel adequate [enough] that I could speak. You know, I didn't have the confidence that they had. . . . It was a class issue.

In many former colonies of Britain, including Muslim countries, access to English has become one method of class differentiation. Zubaida was from a less affluent class than most of the other students at the school. The ease with which the other students, particularly those who belonged to the elites, had adopted English and Western culture was unfamiliar to her. It made her feel more excluded and increased her discomfort around her own ability to speak English. She experienced dissonance between school and home, where Urdu was spoken.[3]

Discomfort with English and westernization lingered, so that Zubaida had mixed feelings about immigrating to Canada:

Zubaida: I think I was feeling scared, and I didn't know what to expect. Leaving all those familiar signs behind, and I think again, maybe the language part.

Shahnaz: What were you afraid of?

Zubaida: People would stare at me, and I was afraid of being spoken to, and again it was the English.

English is still an issue for her. She says that her accent is different, and, therefore, she can be identified as different.

Shahnaz: But we are different.

Zubaida: Right, but you are trying to, I think, assimilate.

Shahnaz: Is that what you are doing?

Zubaida: I think I am.... And I think I have.... I think I felt safer to deny.

Shahnaz: You feel safer to deny what?

Zubaida: Not to feel Pakistani, not look like a Pakistani, and being Muslim is part of it. Also I feel that [being Muslim] has put a lot of restrictions on me personally.

In Canada besides being discriminated against as a woman, Zubaida is also at the nexus of other marginalized locations: the inability to speak English "properly" and being labeled a Pakistani/Muslim. Zubaida connects not being able to speak English with the "proper" accent to being different, or the "other," who is excluded and marginalized. Although her discomfort is occurring in Canada in the 1990s, it is associated with earlier discomfort she experienced as a child in a Pakistani school where she had been marginalized for her "improper" English.

Yet being a Muslim has connotations other than the Orientalist/racist stereotyping from the dominant culture. Being a Muslim also includes the sexual and social control of women perpetuated by their own families and communities. Zubaida remembers different rules at home regarding mobility and education for girls and boys. The girls had little mobility, while the boys had few restrictions. The men in Zubaida's family, in particular her brother, attempted to enforce control of women, both in Canada and in Pakistan. Such control of Muslim women translates into control of the women's morality to ensure the morality of the community. This male responsibility is often connected to men's sense of honor. Quoting an eminent twelfth-century theologian, Abu Hamid Muhammad al-Gazali, Tahire Kocturk (1992, 55) points to a *hadith* in which a man without honor is identified as one who will not go to paradise. The *hadith* goes on to elaborate that this man without honor is one who does not exercise control and guard the chastity of his daughter, wife, mother, or sister. Such a source easily provides justification/motive for men to enforce the honor of their women.

The honor of the "authentic" Muslim woman is connected to issues of embodiment and dress, which Zubaida confronts, negotiates, and resists. Her brother had come to Canada earlier than the rest of the family and wrote advising them what clothes to bring. He particularly asked them not to bring Pakistani clothes but to bring westernized clothes, shirts and pants. Back in Pakistan, Zubaida had been allowed to wear only *shalwar kameez,* and she says she had worn jeans as "a sign of rebellion." Suddenly she found her brother telling her she should wear jeans in Canada. Yet:

> Zubaida: After coming here, we realized how stupid he was because people were wearing these things [*shalwar kameez*], especially in your own home or in summer, and I think I still have the thing in me that I don't feel comfortable wearing *shalwar kameez* outside the home. . . . I mean not at all any more.
>
> Shahnaz: Why?
>
> Zubaida: Not just what he wrote, but I know that women who wear them are targeted. The stuff that is happening in Canada, the racism.

She does not want to be stereotyped as a Muslim/Pakistani woman, and she believes that to some extent she has "assimilated" into Canadian culture.

> Zubaida: Assimilation, I think that is what has happened [to me].
>
> Shahnaz: You now keep your identity for the festive days.
>
> Zubaida: Not even for the festive days; I mean that is where it is at now.

Obedience to a family patriarch usually comes with the protection by the patriarch. This was not always so in Zubaida's home. She realized that although her brother wanted servitude and obedience from her, cooking, keeping the house clean, and not dating, he was not willing to guide her about Canadian institutions, particularly educational systems and procedures.

> Zubaida: I enrolled in two courses. They were psychology courses. . . . But [I] ended up dropping them. It was beyond me. . . . At college I felt that I was thrown into something that I didn't know anything about.
>
> Shahnaz: Were they first-year courses?
>
> Zubaida: They were continuing ed[ucation] courses. I just picked up the calendar for the evening courses, and now looking back I feel quite angry around the way my brother did not come with me. He just told me, "That is where the university office is; go and talk to somebody about admission." I never did things on my own; I didn't know how.
>
> Shahnaz: Why did he not go with you to the office?
>
> Zubaida: I don't know.

Zubaida was not willing to submit to the notion of Muslim female identity as her brothers and father wanted to enact it and began dating a white man.

Shahnaz: What did your family say? Did they know?

Zubaida: They did not know in the beginning. Then I started seeing him more and more.

Shahnaz: Was sexual intimacy part of the relationship?

Zubaida: Yes, it was part of the deal. I am putting things together now to make sense of them because at that time I was so desperate to get out of the house.

Shahnaz: Did you move in with him?

Zubaida: Not right away. I moved out initially to live with my cousin. ... My Mom ... she was strongly against [it] and said, "We are providing everything for you, and why are you complaining?" And stuff. So as the date of my moving out came closer, my father started to say things, and he started to cry. Like "You are giving us a bad name. What will people think?" and all that. And what he did to prove his point is that he left the house. He said that "I can't live here."

He left, she claims, because "not only did he lose control over his family but also over his own life, because he didn't get the jobs that he was used to here." He had not been able to continue the career he had in Pakistan. One day he disappeared from the house. The family hired an investigator and traced him a year later to another province in Canada. Her father's disappearance not only made Zubaida feel "guilty about moving out" and "furious at him for what he had done," but also increased the uncertainty that moving out was supposed to help resolve.

Zubaida moved in with her white boyfriend and tried to work through some of the contradictions in her life.

Shahnaz: Did they [your family] know you were living with a white man before marriage?

Zubaida: Oh, yeah.

Shahnaz: Did that cut you off from them?

Zubaida: Yes. . . . My mother is fine; she likes him; she comes and visits and stays with us.

Shahnaz: Did she approve when you first married?

Zubaida: Yes, with her the issue was that I was getting married. That was a relief to her.

Shahnaz: What about your brothers and your father?

Zubaida: We don't talk because of that.

Zubaida is in a heterosexual relationship, she says, because she was not aware that she had a choice.

Zubaida: I had this . . . expectation that I was going to be in a hetero-sexual relationship. As I was growing up I didn't know much about my own body.

Shahnaz: Where are you at with that right now? Do you still feel that you are heterosexual?

Zubaida: Well, I am married to a man, so I guess. . . . And there are certain things that I do think about in terms of that.

Shahnaz: About women?

Zubaida: Relationships with women, yes, and also marrying a white man, how that had to do with my own need for acceptance in a white society.

Shahnaz: Do you think you have been accepted?

Zubaida: I think I am more accepted. This is my perception. I could be totally wrong, but I think I have, you know, the status elevation that happens. I feel to an extent that has happened. Some things are easier in terms of dealing with the bureaucracy, the university application stuff. I have no experience dealing with university and bureaucracy and the application procedures.

Shahnaz: So he does it for you.

Zubaida: He does it for me. He knows the system, and he has the lan-guage; he has the jargon, but I don't know how it helps me in terms of finding my own ability to do things. I think that is negative, that I am not using my own or developing my own ability to do things.

Shahnaz: What about relationships with women?

Zubaida: I am curious maybe that is something that I could have. . . . I have never been in a relationship with a woman, so I don't know what it is like.

Shahnaz: Do you feel that is something you could explore?

Zubaida: I didn't explore that, and I could have, or I might, who knows.

In trying to move out of the gender and racial inequality of Islam, she moves into the relations of gender and racial inequality of Canadian soci-ety, and it has not been the answer to her independence. Only now is she beginning to realize that she could have had a choice, particularly regard-ing sexual preference. She is not sure what the future will bring.

Zubaida attempts to escape the control of the men in her family and questions acceptance in the larger Canadian culture.

Shahnaz: You talked about denial of being a Pakistani in Canada. What does it mean to you to be a Pakistani that you have to deny it?

Zubaida: I am not proud of it.

Shahnaz: Tell me what that means for you.

Zubaida: After coming here and seeing how people talk about them [Pakistanis] and put them down.

Shahnaz: Do you agree with the stereotypes?

Zubaida: No I don't, I mean the workshop that I was doing in antiracism and the stuff that people have about them.

Shahnaz: But whose fault is that? Is it the fault of the Pakistanis, or is it the fault of the stuff that people have?

Zubaida: The misinformation, the people who are in control of the media and all that.

Shahnaz: What about the people who are accepting the stereotypes?

Zubaida: I don't know. If there is racism, I mean am I to be faulted for it because I am accepting it?

Shahnaz: So you feel that humans don't have any agency?

Zubaida: I feel it is for the most part structural, . . . and I don't know what power I have to change the structure.

Zubaida's comments indicate an acceptance of the inevitability of racism as a structural phenomenon. In admitting powerlessness in the face of structural oppression, she appears unable to contradict the Orientalist categorizations of her life. Zubaida cannot totally accept Orientalist stereotypes about herself except to say there is no alternative but to assimilate. And she cannot identity herself with Islamism either.

When asked about her experiences with the organized "Islamic community" in Canada, she replied:

Zubaida: I went to them in the initial years [un]til 1986. I was attending the meetings of the *Ahmediyia* community here. I wasn't happy when I was there because the thing that I heard were [sic] more sexism, a wish for segregation, and there was hardly any talk around how we adjust as a community to a new country and what kind of things we can do to support each other, or what happens when you don't have jobs, education, or opportunities.

Also, Zubaida had begun to live with the man she would later marry, and this was causing her mother embarrassment. She did not want to make her mother feel uncomfortable. She was afraid.

Zubaida: People will ask questions and stuff like that. I just removed myself from the community because that was her security.

Zubaida had challenged the vision of the authentic Muslim woman. Her cultural/religious community was not able to provide security, guidance, or support for her in part because she was a woman living with a man outside of marriage. So in order not to jeopardize her mother's support from the community, Zubaida opted out of the community.

Although Zubaida asserts she removed herself from the community, recently she was on a committee along with a local imam dealing with issues of Muslim school children. A school board in Toronto had organized the committee, which was constituted of school officials and Muslims, to deal with issues that come up for Muslim students. The imam was Sunni, and because ninety percent of Muslims are Sunni, Zubaida says he claimed he represented ninety percent of the Muslims in Toronto.[4] This imam, according to Zubaida, had authority on this particular committee because of his supposed leadership role in the "Islamic community." Zubaida claims that if this had been any other committee, and especially because of the kinds of statements he was making, he would have been asked to leave. For instance:

> Zubaida: He says . . . girls should not be asked to do certain activities in phys[ical] ed[ucation] because they might break their hymen or because they lose their virginity. . . . I was so emotional that I just said that girls can break their hymen riding their bloody bike, and his answer is don't ride a bike.

By participating on the committee, Zubaida provides an alternate voice from within the "Islamic community." She recognizes the Islamic community as heterogeneous and challenges the imam's right to make pronouncements for all Sunnis. As she speaks out on the committee, Zubaida is contesting the religious authority of the imam to define the category Muslim. Paradoxically, Zubaida is appalled at the sexism in Islamic practices and claims she is no longer Muslim. She claims space for herself as Muslim through a rereading of the recorded codes and negotiates a hybridized Muslim identity in the third space.

Zubaida's testimony suggests other contradictions as well. She believes that people are responsible for their own exclusion, yet feels the need to defend being Pakistani/Muslim against racist and discriminatory remarks.

> Zubaida: On the one hand, I am defending the country and Muslim, and on the other hand I have this anger about it because I know the kind of impact it has had on my personal life.

Moreover, Zubaida's attempts at assimilation as well as rejection of Islam do not necessarily resolve her ambivalent relationship toward Islam or her understanding of herself as Muslim. Although she rejects Islam, she identifies herself as a Muslim feminist because "there are parts of me that I cannot change." She calls herself feminist, is curious about feminist interpretations of *Qur'an*, and would one day like to read them.

Zubaida's account suggests the doubly alienating position of being caught between Orientalism and Islamism. In her attempts to assimilate she is moving into a third space:

> Zubaida: This is also a struggle for me. I mean, I am trying to find my own place in all this in terms of what is happening with, first, the family issues, and moving to Canada and all that, and finding my own identity around racism and all that. . . . I find it easier to reject Islam than to deal with this interpretation and that interpretation.
>
> Shahnaz: What does that do for your identity?
>
> Zubaida: Plays havoc. I don't know, depressing me. I guess, probably I am in a depression of some kind.

Zubaida's myths of home, her family, as well as her experiences with her diasporic community suggest religiously based attempts to control her mobility and sexuality. She also confronts racist/Orientalist myths of the Pakistani/Muslim woman in the dominant culture. Zubaida attempts to resolve the ambivalence she faces through a rejection of the religious determination of Muslim female identify. Yet she does not totally reject the Orientalist construction of the Muslim Other. Although her narrative suggests that she negotiates and translates the politics of Orientalism and Islamism within a third space in Canada, her struggles lead her to despair and depression.

Nikhat

Shortly after I had interviewed Nikhat, I realized that owing to a technical error I had not taped the interview. I tried to contact her, but she was not at the number she had given. I wrote down what she had said as I remembered it. Despite the fact that I do not have transcripts for Nikhat, it is worthwhile making the following observations, because her story provides an example of a woman who is attempting to resolve her relationship to Muslim female identity by saying that she is no longer Muslim and that she is white/European.

Nikhat is a white-skinned, middle-class Turkish woman in her late twenties. She had a "modern" education in Turkey, which focused on differentiating between Turkey and the rest of the Islamic world and moving toward a cultural affinity with Europe.[5] Upon finishing her B.A. in Ankara, she began to work in a bank. Around the same time she also moved out of her parents' home and moved in with her boyfriend. Although they were living together without being married, she had to tell the landlady that they were married; otherwise they could not have rented the apartment. Her immediate family knew that she and her boyfriend were not married, but the extended family did not. Nikhat did not want to embarrass her parents, so she agreed to tell her extended family she was married. She and her boyfriend did decide to get married, but he was killed in a traffic accident a few weeks before the wedding. Although his family had tolerated her when their son was alive, she claims, they did not want to have anything to do with her after his death.

Through her westernized education, Nikhat appears to have internalized Euro-American devaluation of Turkish/Muslim culture. For instance, she complained of the lack of art in Islamic culture. When I reminded her of the rich tradition of Islamic miniature painting, architecture, calligraphy, and so forth, she replied, "but our mosques do not have pictures like they have in Christian churches." Her remark confirmed the centrality of the European church as ideal and desired in its combination of art, architecture, and religion. Nikhat also pointed out that since Turkey was "European," Islamic heritage was not as relevant to her. As Bhabha points out, "In the act of disavowal and fixation the colonial subject is returned to the narcissism of the Imaginary and its identification of an ideal-ego that is white and whole" (1990a, 81). From the fragmented Muslim identity constructed in difference, Nikhat exhibits an almost Lacanian desire for wholeness, which she reads as whiteness.

Nikhat's response suggests a discursive mimicry, ambivalence in which the colonial subject is a partial presence, incomplete, and virtual (Bhabha 1994c, 86). As such, the Turk as colonial subject can be only known through the discourse of the colonizer. Nikhat reiterates this discourse when she claims that as a Turk she is white and is not discriminated against. Those Turks who are discriminated against are fringe Islamic groups and responsible for the exclusion and stereotyping they face. Her response reinforces a class division between the westernized, affluent class in Turkey and the majority of Turks who cannot afford the benefits of westernization. She is part of the Turkish westernized bourgeoisie, which aspires to become part of the European community and whom, as R. Margulies and E. Yildizoglu (1988) point out, many view as having "sold out" to the West. In claiming to be white (that is, European and not Muslim), Nikhat hopes to resolve the ambivalence she feels about herself as a Muslim woman from a devalued culture and history.[6]

Her experience as a student of English in Canada for the last two years, however, suggests that it is not so simple. She is single and supports herself by working as a cleaning lady and as a kitchen helper in a Greek restaurant. Nikhat has been sexually harassed at the restaurant and feels unable to do anything about it. If she complains, she thinks that she will lose her job, and she needs the money. Nikhat's experiences at the restaurant have taught her that not all westernized women are safe from sexism. She has come to believe that freedom for women in Canada exists only in a certain respect and only for certain women. If you are different-looking or have a different name, you are treated as an outcast. She is not sure that she can deal with this form of discrimination.

In Canada her attempts at resolution through claims of whiteness/ Europeanness produce further ambivalence. She is not treated as white/ European but is categorized as a Turk/Muslim Other and confronts the structured ambivalence in the often contradictory determinations of Muslim female identity. Because of her experiences of exclusion and devaluation in Canada, Nikhat claimed she was extremely depressed. Her education and her experience have not been recognized, and she does not see a future for herself in Canada. When I met Nikhat, she had recently been in contact with her former employers in Turkey. They had told her that since her English had improved by living in Canada, they were willing to take her back at the bank at a higher position than she had before. Nikhat was seriously considering going back to Turkey. I lost track of her. Perhaps she is back in Turkey, where westernization in a Turkish Muslim woman "pays off" much better than in Canada.

Safieh, Zubaida, and Nikhat are translating codes and categories of prescriptions and description into everyday rituals of collusion and resistance in the third space. They disavow themselves as Muslims and so attempt to resolve the structural ambivalence that being coded as Muslim evokes. Yet the disavowal does not produce the resolution to their dissonance. Instead they find that they to some extent not only continue to be coded as Muslim and be responded to as Muslim by others, but they themselves also react as Muslim.

4

Negotiating the Ambivalence

The women in this chapter—Iram, Rabia, Ayesha, Karima, Mussarat, Zahra, Kausar, and Nabia—appear to have accepted religious and cultural rituals as one operative norm of the "authentic" Muslim woman. They are fully aware that their lives cannot subscribe to ideas of perceived authenticity for Muslim women because of the following factors: the changing vision of the authentic; their own rejection of the sexism in Islamic practices; the economic and social reality of the 1990s; and finally, the exclusion and devaluation they face in Canada. Acceptance of different, often antagonistic, visions of Muslim female identity places women in a no-win situation. Since they cannot subscribe to all they have accepted as authentic, for many guilt becomes a response to the situation.

These contradictions position individual women in a space to which they respond with dissonance. The contradictory nature of this discourse impacts on women in a way that never lets them totally escape. In terms of being a Muslim woman, they are "in" but not in, and "out" but not quite out. Their narratives suggest oppositional as well as nonoppositional positions to their discursive locations. They respond to notions of authentic Muslim woman and often narrate received views of home. Yet their narratives also suggest that "home" is the site of the mundane daily life in Canada.

The contradictions in the categorization of the Islamic female necessarily produce a structured ambivalence. Even those women who do not experience emotional dissonance confront this structured ambivalence. Women respond to the ambivalence with an emotional dissonance that is frequently mutually alienating and not always logical. Dissonance is thus a response to the contradictions, and ambivalence is structured around the contradictory discourses embedded in Muslim women's identity. Women confront these key concepts when they negotiate their identity in

Canada. In this third space women confront dialectic polarities, and as hybridized individuals they forge new positionalities for themselves as Muslim, a mestiza consciousness where they turn their contradictions into strength.

This chapter explores aspects of ambivalence along a continuum, beginning with Iram, who faces contradictions but does not express any dissonance. Rabia is clear about the contradictions she faces, yet she expresses some emotional dissonance. Mussarat, Ayesha, Karima, Zahra, Kausar, and Nabia experience emotional dissonance and disharmony. Their narratives suggest that although they negotiate their lives as hybridized subject, to an extent they also accept the authority of monolithic notions of Islam and Orientalist views regarding what the Muslim woman is.

Iram

Born in Uganda, of East Indian background, Iram has been in Canada since she was four. She is brown-skinned and twenty-four years old. Iram's few memories of Uganda center around her father physically and verbally abusing their male domestic. Her identity appears to have been shaped by her life in Canada, and she recalls that her father treated her mother and her sisters as he did the servant back "home." She also remembers the racism that her older sister faced as they were growing up, particularly when Iram was six and her sister was eight. The boys at school would call her sister "Paki" and "Punjab," and Iram used to rush to defend her. Iram did not suffer the same racism because, she says, she was more aggressive. "I also remember beating up a kid who was significantly older than me on the way to school one day when he was trying to pick on my sister. So people knew that I wasn't afraid of these guys." Iram and her sisters did not tell their parents what was going on in school because they were afraid of their father, and because their mother had enough to deal with. Iram believes that the racial harassment at school occurred because of her family's name, and skin color, and because of cultural stereotyping. Being Muslim did not make a difference at school until Iram chose to emphasize it.

Iram claims that she was confronted in high school by considerable Western mythology about Islam largely because of the 1979 Iranian revolution. She recalls that while other students were either too embarrassed or too afraid to identify themselves as Muslims, she began to emphasize her Muslim difference. Iram believes this is because she is a rebel.

Iram: Everybody always said Khomeini was a crazy man, an "asshole," a terrorist. Terrorist was the key word. I would point out that he was maybe a terrorist, but you have got terrorists all over the world. Why aren't you calling the IRA terrorist? Why don't you go back in Canadian history and find out who in Canada was a terrorist? Then I particularly talked about American terrorists around the world. I remember very clearly I had a locker across from another girl's, and in her locker she hung an American flag. I was so incensed by that, that in my locker I hung a poster. . . . It depicted basically an airplane with two wings. On one wing was a Soviet emblem, on another wing was an American flag, and in the middle was a hand with an Islamic crescent crushing both of them. . . . And in the background were Muslim women and men with their hands raised up in the air, with their fists clenched. In the background was Arabic writing, and I can't remember what it said.

The vice principal was passing by our lockers one day. He saw this [poster] in mine. He said that I had to take it down. I said no, I would not. He said, "You have to. This is ridiculous. This is propaganda and terrorism, and I asked him to turn around, and I pointed to the American flag in that girl's locker. First of all, I told him how I felt about the very fact that represented the same thing to me, and I told him that until she takes that down, I will not take this down. And he said "I am afraid that your interpretation is very skewed, and you know that you are just going to have to take it down." I reiterated to him why I wouldn't, and I said that if he wanted to take it to the school board, I would be very happy to show up at the school board and debate this in front of him. He knew that he was not getting across to me, so he just left it at that.

Iram's rebellious spirit also caused conflict at a school of Islamic religious instruction that she attended as a child. She was permanently expelled for asking too many questions and insisting on answers. Blind faith was not enough for her. Currently Iram works as a journalist for a mainstream publication, and her work environment provides her with ample opportunities to confront people about their views on Islam. Iram claims that her employers and co-workers actually listen to what she has to say although they do not always agree with her:

Iram: Well for example, just this past Friday in memory of December sixth, I wrote an article on abuse that women face in Canada. . . . I specifically blasted the paper for running a feature last summer on "Women behind the Veil: Back to Fundamentalist Islam in a Male Dominated Society." . . . And I pointed out in that article of mine that, sure, abuse goes on in Islamic countries, but keep in mind that it goes on all over the world. Let's look at Canada. And I pointed out all the different abuses that happen in Canada. I made it very, very clear that I was not denying the pain that women face in Islamic countries. What I am denying is, [the notion that] it is worse than it is in Canada.

Iram has lived in Canada since age four and learned to defend herself early in life. As a child she suffered emotional and physical abuse and racial harassment. Her childhood memories include those of her father physically and verbally abusing her, her sisters, and their mother, as well as the racism that she and her sisters faced at school. Iram was subjected to stereotyping and racism not because she was identified as Muslim but because people responded to her as South Asian or East Indian.[1]

Iram: In the early seventies most people didn't know the difference between being Muslim and being just plain brown. All they could see was your name and your skin color, and they immediately assumed that you were some sort of Indian who ate curry all the time.

Being East Indian in Canada, as I have argued elsewhere (Khan 1991), often means being seen as inferior and belonging to a decadent culture and civilization. Being a Muslim became an issue both to Iram and those around her at school because, as the political climate surrounding Muslims and Islam changed, Iram emphasized it.

Shahnaz: When did being Muslim start making a difference, if it ever did?

Iram: Let me make one thing clear, that if it ever made a difference, it was because I emphasized the difference.

Shahnaz: Why did you feel the need to emphasize it?

Iram: It probably started making a difference for me in high school. . . . There was enough Western-promoted mythology about Islam thanks to the [Irani] revolution. If I did bring it up, there would be a whole new series of attacks on me.

Shahnaz: Why would you bring it up?

Iram: Because I was very proud to be Muslim.

Shahnaz: What made you proud of something that people thought was negative?

Iram: Keep in mind that I was always a rebel. Remember that ever since I was five years old [if] somebody said dark, I would say light. So the fact that people had negative images of Islam just drove into me the need to raise it and to educate people.

Iram is brown and can be phenotypically othered. Her visibly racial location as South Asian compounds with her defense of Islam as a "religion of terrorists" in a political climate in which the "Islamic threat" horrifies popular imagination.

Shahnaz: Were you called a . . . terrorist in high school?

Iram: Even though racism was clear, I never was the overt target of it. A lot of people respected me, because I did speak out. I was very involved in the school, so personally I never was called a terrorist, but my religion was called terrorism.

Shahnaz: And that made you angry?

Iram: It made me angry, not because I denied it. I never denied that there was terrorism. What I denied was that this [Islam] was the only bastion of terrorism.

Angered by what she encounters, Iram turns away from Orientalist/racist construction of her identity. Yet she finds that she cannot restructure herself in what Islam appears to offer. Her experiences with the fundamentalist influenced and organized Islamic/Shia community in Vancouver provide an example:

Iram: I remember when I was twelve or thirteen being kicked out, permanently from Saturday school.

Shahnaz: Why?

Iram: Because I asked too many questions.

Shahnaz: About what?

Iram: About everything. When the teacher was teaching, let's say about Islamic history, I would say Why this? Why that? Why didn't Khadija do this? . . . And at one point he told me, "Look, either you believe what I say or you get out."

Shahnaz: So pure faith on the basis of "what I say" was not enough?

Iram: Well, I shut up for a while. Then I started to ask questions again because things didn't make sense to me, and I wanted to know. And I got so angry with the fact that he became so angry with me that I said, "This is it. If you are not going to answer my questions, and if you are going to invalidate my questions, then I don't think that I have a place here." And I walked out. He [the teacher] symbolized the organized aspect of Islam. Always, always, always, I have always had a very deep respect for Islam in its purest form.

Shahnaz: So what do you respect?

Iram: I respect the fact that to me it is almost like a utopia, like communism, which I respect in theory. Islam in its purest form will never be attained, can never be attained.

Iram appears to rebel against the loaded categorization of "Muslim" and what that might entail. Instead, her very insistence that she is a rebel suggests that she at once accepts what conventional definitions of Muslim might mean and refuses to acquiesce to those definitions. To a large extent, Iram is living her life according to what makes sense to her outside of the accepted codes of "Muslim." Yet she is not able to speak to the space she creates in her life. Instead, by placing Islam into the realm of utopia and unlivable, she appears to be suggesting that she can practice progressive politics only outside the category "Muslim."

Iram's disenchantment with members of the organized Islamic/Shia community in Vancouver was reinforced by the way in which they reacted to her parents' divorce. Iram realized that despite the abuse her mother was suffering, the men at the mosque were more interested in keeping the family unit together. She claims they "tried to scuttle the divorce proceedings on more than one occasion." Patriarchal leaders appeared in Iram's view to be more interested in maintaining an image of an ideal Islamic community where divorce does not occur and where the systemic nature of abuse in the family is disavowed. Such views ignore the abuse individuals suffer and attribute it to the pathology of the people involved.

Influenced by family trauma and feminism, Iram claims she became "an activist and very defiant." It dawned on her that the religion that she was defending was very sexist.

Iram: I didn't drop it, mind you, but I became far more critical of religion, far more critical.

Although Iram continues to react to prejudice against Islam because of the sexism that she experienced, she became selective concerning which aspects of religion she would enact in her own life.

Iram: I have a real aversion to organized anything. So I pick and choose from Islam what I want to do and what I want to practice, . . . what I agree with and understand.

In an attempt to anchor her identity, Iram turns away from Orientalism and goes back to the only option she believes is available to her, Islamism. But she contains it in theory and cannot bring it to her everyday life.

Shahnaz: When you say "Islam to me, it is a theoretical thing; it is not something which is lived in my day-to-day life," how would you consider lived Islam in a day-to-day life?

Iram: If I were to call myself a practicing Muslim?

Shahnaz: I am not saying that. That is a particular category.

Iram: But I would have to say this in order to answer the question. I would pray five times a day; I would wear the *hejab;* I would do this, and I would do that.

Shahnaz: So you are defining being Muslim within the traditional tenets.

Iram: That is right.

Shahnaz: But nothing else that you do has been defined within the traditional tenets. Why are you defining this?

Iram: Because that is all I know. I have had this debate before. And even though I am not willing to exclude my Muslim upbringing from my identity, I am also not willing to call myself a Muslim.

Shahnaz: If you define [being a Muslim] in a very narrow sense, then obviously you will have to exclude your day-to-day life.

Iram: Yes, yes.

She separates herself from the "practicing Muslim woman," who for Iram wears the *hejab,* prays five times a day, and lives her life within the traditional tenets of Islam. Her comments affirm the notion of authentic Muslim presented in religious terms, which she affirms in principle but does not live in practice. Iram does not raise this contradiction, she just lives it. Because she cannot accept the sexism in Islam, she cannot be a practicing Muslim. Yet she will not let go of Islam, but she cannot articulate a space in which to restructure her identity in Canadian society, which racializes Muslims. She will defend Islam, she says, the way she defends her brown skin and only with non-Muslims. She feels free to criticize Islam only among Muslims.

Iram: When a white person raises objections toward Islam, I immediately jump to Islam's defense. I always point out that in theory this is what I agree with. . . . [However,] when one of my uncles or one of my relatives or somebody I know who is a Muslim jumps to Islam's defense in terms of sexism, I immediately start criticizing Islam.

She believes in Islam at the ideological level, but because of the sexism and inequality it reproduces, she does not want to have anything to do with it in her life. Such a contradiction expresses the complexity of her relationship to Islamic identity. Racism and anti-Muslim sentiment appear to make Iram support Islam defensively and aggressively and raise the question, How much would she have need to fight for Islam if Canada had not been such an anti-Muslim society? Perhaps she may not have severed her connection to Islam if she were living in a Muslim society. She may have just lived it differently.[2] In Canada, the space for struggle is restricted by an anti-Muslim society and within beleaguered Muslim communities. The restrictions no doubt reinforce Iram's options for living the identity but cannot be definitively stated to be the cause of her retaining her Muslim identity.

Leila Ahmed notes that after having lived in the United States, she realizes that Arabs and Muslims feel almost compelled to take the defensive stance even though they are aware of the gender inequalities rampant in Islamic societies: "despite America's heavy embroilment in the area, and despite the fact that Muslims constitute something like one quarter of the world's population: it is, rather that Americans 'know,' and know without even having to think about it, that the Islamic peoples— Arabs, Iranians, whatever they call themselves—are backward, uncivilized peoples totally incapable of rational conduct. This is overwhelmingly the attitude of the media and of the society at large and also, unfortunately, often that of the smaller groups supposedly representing American informed opinion" (Ahmed 1982, 522).

Miseducation is responsible for the stereotypes of Muslims, Iram states. She has tried to correct and educate people since she was in school and claims that she "would try to debunk some of the images they had of Islam."

As Iram educates people about Islam, she also positions herself as a lesbian. She has "come out" to her family and in her community of friends. She does not see any contradiction between being a Muslim and being a lesbian. She states that there are no suras (verses) in the *Qur'an* forbidding homosexuality, although she admits that the focus and tone of the *Qur'an* is clearly heterosexual.[3] Initially, Iram's mother had mixed feelings about her sexual orientation and had tried to impose some degree of sexual control on Iram according to perceived notions of Islamic mothering. Iram claims, however, that because her mother was never happy in her own marital relationship, she particularly wanted her children to be happy in theirs. She has told Iram that if being a lesbian makes her happy, then she is willing to accept it. As for the religious aspect:

Iram: I don't think Allah has it out for me.

Shahnaz: So you feel you can have a relationship with God and have a relationship with a woman at the same time?

Iram: Absolutely.

Shahnaz: And you think there is no contradiction?

Iram: And I believe that Allah believes that, too. I really do.

Iram is not ambivalent about the contradictions she lives. She knows what she wants out of Islam, and it is not what Islamists advocate for the Muslim woman. Her ambivalence is more of a response to the structural contradictions, for she does not express any emotional dissonance. She is comfortable with her position as she self-identifies with feminism and Western values.

Iram claims that although her mother is an important influence in her life, there is a spiritual difference between them. Her mother is a Muslim, while Iram is a woman who happened to be raised in a Muslim home. If she had a choice, she would not have chosen to be raised in Islam or any other religion. She was raised a Muslim, and since she has never walked away from what she considers a relevant battle, and because she has grown up in Canada fighting, she will fight for Islam.

> Iram: The fact that I didn't think that there was anything wrong with having been brought up Muslim, that I was so angry toward racism itself, you know, and that I was so proud of who I am and what I am. And for that matter if this country is really going to stop being so hypocritical, . . . lauding multiculturalism when it is convenient and blasting it when it is not, . . . I have to be allowed to be who and whatever the hell I want to be.

In the context of racism and Islamphobia, Iram's desire to maintain some kind of Muslim identity inevitably leads her to confront how the Muslim woman is constructed. Iram disavows Islam as a day-to-day practice, but her narrative makes an argument for the way in which the structure of racism produces an investment in the identity of Muslim woman.

> Iram: You know, I am caught right in the middle when it comes to racism and sexism, and for that matter homophobia. . . . When any of this stuff comes up, I feel the urge to come to the battle and fight for it.

Iram's response indicates mutually alienating positions. The positions seem contradictory, yet Iram does not experience confusion or uncertainty about asserting those contradictions. Thus, there is structure of ambivalence (in Bhabha's terms) within that response, an ambivalence that is necessarily an inherent response to the contradictions within the space for Muslim woman herself.

Iram grew up in Canada, and unlike Karima does not have what Bhabha (1994c) would call sustaining myths of a past Muslim identity she once performed and then imported to Canada. Her relationship to home has been transmitted to her by her family and family's social and cultural community. Much of what "home" constitutes she rejects because of the sexism and because of the leap of faith she feels is required of her. Reference to home cannot ease the pain of racism and religious fundamentalism. Instead she appears intensely aware that home is in Canada and that she must carve her space out here.

In primary school Iram was made aware that she was "brown" and different, and since high school, she has chosen to emphasize her Muslim difference. It is significant that these are the two points of her identity that she articulates and defends. I realize that because of the way ethnicity is linked according to geographical, cultural, and political space, Iram may find it difficult to be accepted as a Ugandan in Canada, or indeed in Uganda itself as a Ugandan. However, her narrative could have emphasized a South Asian identity. Instead she chooses to identify herself as part of a religious collective. Although she resists the pressures of what she believes it entails, in negotiating a Muslim identity Iram appears to have accepted the "Islam equals religion" equation.

Rabia

Rabia is brown-skinned and came to Canada from Hyderabad in 1973, when she was twenty-two.[4] She was part of the Muslim elite in Hyderabad who, as Shahida Latif (1990) points out, received westernized education. The school Rabia attended had been set up by Australian and British missionaries and was based on the English model. Indian history was studied from European books, which stressed the benevolence of colonial rule. Although Rabia now looks at it critically, as a child she just accepted Western influences as the better direction for her life, instead of focusing on her own cultural heritage. She recalls: "You just heard and you accepted it. . . . They did not allow anything Eastern." Her social group consisted of children who attended this school as well. They all imitated European ways. The school uniform was a skirt. In India, Rabia says, it is considered immodest for girls to show their legs, so she wore socks up to the hem of her uniform to cover hers.

The population of girls at the school was fifty percent Muslim and fifty percent Hindu. The school administration did not include either Muslim or Hindu cultural/religious studies because of, they said, the antagonisms between people of these religions. Instead they taught Christianity. The students had to learn the Christian gospels, and if they did not pass that subject, they were not promoted to the next class.

Rabia believes that Christianity was a big influence in her life, and Christmas in particular was a big event:

> Rabia: *Eid* was not the same thing.[5] Christmas seemed more fun . . .
> because *Eid* was just an ordinary affair, and there wasn't any Christmas
> tree or gifts being exchanged. You didn't see that happening at *Eid*. . . .
> My children now say, "You know, we should have *Eid* like Christmas.
> We would enjoy it with gifts and lights."

Rabia recalls that she, her family, and others in her milieu took being
Muslim for granted in Hyderabad, while they considered learning and
emulating European culture to be a status-giving attribute. Although the
India in which Rabia grew up was no longer a British colony, the superiority of European culture over Indian culture was a main theme in the
books she read at the missionary school she attended.

> Shahnaz: And what did these books tell you about Indian history?

> Rabia: I am sure a lot of things were misrepresented. You know they
> always try to present Britishers, you know the Europeans as the good
> ones. . . . At that time I didn't even think about it. I think as you mature
> you think about all these things. You thought you had to live the West-
> ern way.

> Shahnaz: Tell me how you thought you had to live.

> Rabia: The one thing was that you were totally taken away from was
> your own language. You thought English was the language, and if you
> don't speak English properly, that was a shame.

> Shahnaz: That was in the school?

> Rabia: School and probably the people I was associating with, since they
> were all coming from the middle-class background. So we were all
> stressing on English. . . . And everything Western was supposed to be
> better than your own culture, you know everything that is good.

> Shahnaz: Like what?

> Rabia: Like they are more organized; they are better people. . . . The way
> they do things is far superior than anything that you do.

> Shahnaz: Were there any specifics, or was it just a general message?

> Rabia: Generally, the impression that anything that belongs to the West
> is far better than our own culture. There was nothing specific. It was in
> the whole system, and you just heard about it, and you accepted it.

Messages "of how people perceived themselves and their relationship to
the world" (Ngugi 1989, 16) help control the mental universe of the colonial child. Rabia is increasingly aware of this "piece of the oppressor,"
which Paulo Freire (1968) states is planted deep within us. Rabia points
out that people who had not gone to these schools "often commented,
'Look at them aping the West,' which was true, now that I think about it."

Rabia notes that English was emphasized at her school and in her social milieu, and only at home was Urdu given any importance.

Shahnaz: Do you think you lost anything else with the language?

Rabia: In a way some of my culture, like some of the values that I think I should attach more importance to.

Shahnaz: Like what?

Rabia: Like the lifestyle. I should emphasize that my own lifestyle has been influenced by the Western way. . . . We always thought in the Western way.

Shahnaz: Tell me how.

Rabia: Like we were not as conservative as a Muslim family. . . . I could wear sleeveless [*kameez*], my mother never objected to anything. . . . And I could wear a dress if I wanted to.

As Fanon writes, such a colonized person, in whom a cultural inferiority has been instilled, is "elevated above his [*sic*] jungle status in proportion to his adoption of the mother country's cultural standards. He becomes whiter as he renounces his blackness, his jungle" (1967, 18).

Although a Muslim in Hindu-dominated India, Rabia's knowledge of English and European culture reinforced her class privilege. Having little knowledge of Urdu or Islam was not an issue for her.

When she immigrated to Canada, she initially believed that her acceptance of westernization and the accompanying socialization through school and her social milieu would help her integrate with life here. "I knew the language. I knew the culture, the religion," she pointed out. The reality, however, was quite different. Rabia's brown skin and categorization as a South Asian, along with her identification as a Muslim, combined to produce her multilayered location in Canada. In this location she was marginalized, excluded, and discriminated against in employment. Her story provides a testimony to her growing awareness and disenchantment with the messages she had received and accepted through her colonial education.

Rabia: I think initially it didn't sink in. You know how it is when you come to a new country: you are excited to see something different, naturally. It is a beautiful country. In India I took social sciences and sociology and English literature. And I did a typing course before I came here, because most people said if you have typing skills, it would help in finding something. So I did have typing skills, but when I came here, I realized that those skills didn't really matter.

Shahnaz: What mattered?

Rabia: What mattered was basically your skin color and your accent. . . . When I went to [job] interviews, . . . people would be saying, "Beg your pardon," constantly, and I said, "What was I doing wrong?"

The racist exclusion that Rabia began to experience in trying to negotiate the workplace relations of Canadian society can be traced back to the marginalizing effect of Orientalism, in particular to the exclusion the colonial woman confronts.[6] At interviews, she claims, the first question was always "Where are you from?" At the time Rabia wore her hair braided, and one man gave her a piece of advice: if she wanted a job she should cut her hair.

Rabia: I was really shocked [at his remark], because I wasn't expecting something like that, and I was so new to the country, and at the time I didn't have the confidence to come out and say, "What do you mean by that?" . . . I really felt kind of . . . not very good about myself at the time. I said [to myself] "Is there something lacking or wrong with me, if I don't have hair which are [sic] cut?" . . . Now, I could braid my hair and go to an interview, and if he asked me I would turn around and tell them if they don't like it, tough. But at that time I was too young, too inexperienced, and I came home and told my husband, and he said, "You have to make that decision whether you want to really cut your hair to get a job. Because I am not going to impose [it] on you." But I did cut my hair.

Shahnaz: Why?

Rabia: I think, it was the pressure to conform.

Shahnaz: Did you get a job?

Rabia: No.

Thus, even attempts at conformity were no assurance of gaining material rewards. In fact, when she did find work as a receptionist, Rabia discovered she was being paid less than the other staff for doing the same work.

Rabia: There was a black woman who was working with me. She asked me, "How much are they paying you?" I said, "One hundred dollars a week," or something. She said, "Why did you accept it?" I said, "What choice do I have?"

Rabia's coworker pressured her into going to ask the boss for a raise. She recalls:

Rabia: I did go in there. . . . I was very shy about it. With Eastern culture you are not really supposed to be aggressive. A woman is not supposed to be aggressive. I told him, "I don't think it is fair," and I said, "The others make more than I do, and I am doing the same work." He did give me a raise. It wasn't much, but at least I felt better about it, that I had accomplished something.

Such incidents illustrate that Rabia's oppression is multilayered. She is a woman, South Asian, and Muslim and suffers a triple disadvantage. Her acceptance of the view that "Eastern" culture emphasizes women's roles as passive helps sustain stereotypes about South Asian women. Such determinations allow employers to exploit women from what are considered more "traditional" cultures, providing another example of "Eastern" sexism being reinforced and exploited by "Western" sexism and racism.

Rabia and her husband moved to Saudi Arabia in 1981, and there she learned to experience her life as a Muslim. As Rabia observed, she had in some sense more freedom to be herself in Saudi Arabia than in Canada.

Shahnaz: If you talk to most people, they would say that in Saudi Arabia there is a lot less freedom for women than here. Would you agree?

Rabia: Freedom in the Western sense, yes. [In Saudi Arabia] you are not allowed to drive, not allowed to work. You can work as a teacher or as a doctor in segregated workplaces, but not otherwise.

Shahnaz: Then how was there more freedom for you there than here?

Rabia: There is more freedom here, definitely. Freedom of movement. But as a person I didn't really feel restricted [in Saudi Arabia.] . . . I could say what I wanted to.

Shahnaz: What about Islamic restrictions in Saudi Arabia? You can't drive.

Rabia: Which is not really Islamic. . . . I think it is just the culture, not Islam. That bothered me. But the other restrictions didn't bother me, like covering the hair. I think that is the way the people were. I think you have to sometimes conform to the laws of the country. . . . If you are going downtown in Saudi Arabia, you don't wear tight jeans. . . . You are going to dress in a way that you don't show your body so much, . . . and it didn't really bother me.

Shahnaz: Did you wear a *dupatta* on the head?

Rabia: Not all the time. It depended. Basically through Ramadan, I did through the month of fasting, because they did expect people to observe. . . . I learned a lot about religion when I went to Saudi Arabia. . . . The basic things about Islam are very good in Saudi Arabia.

Shahnaz: What sort of things?

Rabia: The whole environment was Muslim. When people heard the azan, they would stop right away.[7] If you were in the car, you stop and start praying. Everyone is praying, and all the shops are closed. In India I came from a Muslim home, but in my environment at school or outside the home I never experienced anything like this, especially [since] I was a minority in India.

Shahnaz: What else did you experience that gave you a sense of being a Muslim?

Rabia: Well, the fasting. The whole month of Ramadan, you would feel the festivities in the air, and the shops were closed. It is the best time of the year. It was such an attractive way of getting you to fast.

Shahnaz: What was an attractive way?

Rabia: Just the environment. The shops were closed during the day, and they would open in the evening for *iftar*.[8] It was pressure because everyone else was doing it, and that is the main thing. Everyone else is doing it, and you do it, too. There was [sic] a lot of people giving *zakat*,[9] especially in Mecca, and rich Saudis serve food free at *iftar,* and most of the mosques have free food. Rich Saudis would have food catered at the mosque. You can have a delicious *iftar,* and it was lovely.

Shahnaz: Did you go to the mosque?

Rabia: Yes I did. It is different from India. Women go to the mosque regularly. I went with the family pretty often, at least once a week, which I had never done in India. I felt a spiritual feeling going to the mosque, which I had never had in India.

When in 1991 Rabia moved back to Canada, she found, once again, that as a Muslim she was discriminated against and devalued.

Rabia: Before, when I had been in Canada, I hadn't felt the racism and discrimination on the basis of religion. I had not been aware of it, and it was a disappointment that again I am [sic] facing the same process of being accepted. In a way it was like being in India, where westernization was valued and being Muslim was dismissed, except that I was aware this time. I felt demoralized and out of place. In Saudi Arabia it was such a secure thing to be a Muslim, and now you were not accepted again.

Shahnaz: Did it make you more determined to be accepted as a Muslim?

Rabia: As a Muslim and [as one] not conforming to the Western concepts and religion in all aspects. I also wanted to be accepted as a woman, as a wife, and in particular as a mother. Most important [was] the mother.

Shahnaz: How would you like to have this happen?

Rabia: That my children become proud of their identity, and become believing and practicing Muslims.

Her increasing awareness of being Muslim appears connected to her reclaiming of Islamic identity. Rabia reiterates her commitment and motivation in not only maintaining the Muslim identity that she discovered in Saudi Arabia but in imparting it to her children as well.

Shahnaz: How do you want your children to live their lives as Muslims?

Rabia: I want them to fast, pray. Yes, I do impose it on my children.

Shahnaz: What about freedom for your children?

Rabia: I have the trust, but I am scared of the environment as well. My kids haven't completely been raised here either. Their foundation has been in Saudi Arabia, so, it is more traditional. I may not have as big a problem as [other parents have] with other Muslim kids.

Shahnaz: What kinds of problems?

Rabia: I don't believe in premarital sex. I think I would have a hard time accepting it . . . with both children.

Shahnaz: And if they decide to do it, what would you do?

Rabia: Now if it comes to that, Shahnaz, we don't have that much control. I know if she [daughter] comes and tells me, or he [son] comes and tells me after eighteen, "You can't make this decision for me," I am going to sit down and talk to them, definitely. And if they don't listen, then I can't do anything about it.

Shahnaz: So you will accept it.

Rabia: I will have to accept it, even though I don't like it. . . . I have brought them to this country; they are in an alien culture. So they are under a lot of stress. They have to conform to a lot of things. There is peer pressure at school, so basically I have put them through all this. It is a hard thing for the children, the stereotypes, the ignorance. Although I find that living in Saudi Arabia has had a very positive impact on my children. My son, he [is] very proud of being a Muslim. . . . My daughter seems to have more problems than my son [has]. I think her identity is still not completely formed. She is fourteen, and she is going through a hard time. It has been a very big adjustment for her. It is a totally different lifestyle from Saudi Arabia. . . . She is confused, and she might have a harder time than my son. I am scared, and I just hope that she will find the right way and find what is good for her.

Being a Muslim mother is an important role to Rabia, and she would like to be supported. Yet she is not getting this support from the Islamic community that she has encountered through her work in community services. Instead she faces issues of authenticity:

Shahnaz: The organized Islamic communities in Toronto: what are your feelings and what are your experiences about them?

Rabia: I am nct really a follower of traditional Islam, . . . which is "Women should be doing this," . . . "They shouldn't work," . . . "They should stay at home," and all those things. And "You should not wear skirts," and "You should not be going out." . . . To me all those things [are] ritual [more] than really the true sense of Islam.

Shahnaz: What do you consider religion?

Rabia: Religion, I consider it is my relationship with God, and being a Muslim is, I think, accepting some of the concepts of Islam, like fasting [and] praying. Praying, too, you don't have to really pursue. I know that a lot of people may not agree with me, but I have to pray when I feel that I have to pray. It is my relationship with Allah. Nobody can tell me, "You have to do this."

Rabia accepts from the prescriptions what she believes and what makes sense to her. She is clear that she does not have to follow all the rules she encounters within community forums. Her interest lies in her own relationship with God. She does not attempt to reconcile the contradictions of the Muslim woman. Instead she decides which rituals define her as Muslim.

As she confronts these unreconcilable expectations for the authentic Muslim woman, Rabia voices tenuous support of feminism:

Rabia: To be honest, I haven't been exposed to it. . . . I did not learn about it in my missionary school or in Saudi Arabia, which is totally patriarchal. . . . Feminism to me is women who say "We are liberated, we are free, we do what we want, we think the way we want to, and men should be condemned." To me, that is the message I get.

Shahnaz: From where do you get this message?

Rabia: From radio talks . . . from the media, from the people around . . .

Rabia realizes that popular media images of Muslim women are problematic, and when I questioned her about the nature of media coverage of feminism, she conceded that perhaps their images of feminists are also biased. She reiterated her support for women's struggles yet stated that she was not an extreme person and that she suspected feminism might be a form of extremism. Although Rabia claims such concerns are due to a fear of being labelled "antimale," they could also be due to the suspicion with which feminism is held in the "Third World" and in Islamic countries.[10]

Despite her misgivings about feminism, Rabia supports women's rights and equality for women. When confronted by the prospect of having *Shari'a* for Muslims in Canada, she seemed unsure:

Shahnaz: What do you think about that, having *Shari'a* law here [in Canada]?

Rabia: I am not sure about that really. I don't think it would really work.

Shahnaz: Why not?

Rabia: I would have to think about it.

Shahnaz: What are the pros and cons?

Rabia: In some ways I find it good. . . . When you are talking about *Shari'a* law, you are talking about divorce.

Shahnaz: What about divorce?

Rabia: According to *Shari'a* law you can get divorced.

Shahnaz: According to Canadian law you can get divorced.

Rabia: But there is the sharing of property, fifty / fifty.

Shahnaz: And you don't think women should have fifty / fifty?

Rabia: Depending on the situation . . . I don't think all women put so much into a marriage. . . . And I am all for women getting their share . . . although they do say in *Shari'a* that a woman keeps whatever she brings in.

Shahnaz: What if a woman doesn't bring anything to the marriage? What if she only works in the house? What then?

Rabia: That was considered in Islam. If it [divorce] did happen, the community would support her.

Shahnaz: Is there such a community here?

Rabia: There is no community, so here it cannot apply. It can only apply in places where the community is really taking the responsibility.

Rabia appeared to experience some hesitation in totally rejecting the request to have *Shari'a* in Canada. She argued that *Shari'a* was part of the community structure in which men were obliged to look after their mothers and their unmarried sisters. I pointed out that such close communities do not always exist in Muslim countries and do not exist at all in Canada. Therefore, the divorce settlement—which favors men, such as the one advocated by *Shari'a*, without the compulsory obligations for the brothers and sons toward their sisters and mothers—does not make sense. Rabia argued that such communities existed only during the life of the Prophet and admitted that *Shari'a* was probably "man" made. She found it difficult, however, to criticize it, perhaps because she would be labeled "too" assertive.

In not totally accepting *Shari'a* or the visions of authenticity for the Muslim women as advocated by those who draw upon religion to imagine a social order, Rabia speaks from a position that is in part outside that supported by many members of organized Islamic communities. Yet to instill a Muslim identity in her children, she will need some community structures. Instead of support, Rabia faces questions of authenticity within the Islamic communities, and she expresses concern about her ability to impart a Muslim identity to her children without that support.

> Rabia: I find it is too isolated [in Canada]. I fear for my children. I came here when I was secure, I was confident, I was grounded. My children are not grounded.

Rabia's myths of home from India position her as a westernized Indian. Yet in Canada her Europeanness was not validated. Like many other minorities (including Nikhat) she was excluded from and devalued in mainstream society. She discovered another set of myths about her Muslimness in Saudi Arabia. There she fit in again and felt included. On returning to Canada she found no space for herself either in mainstream society or in the organized Islamic communities. So she negotiates her own determinations of myths and location. Rabia may have grounded herself in the rituals she performed in Saudi Arabia, but her children have their own translations and negotiations in the third space. Their reiterations are different, and Rabia fears that their vision is not the same as hers. But they do not have the same relationship to India or Saudi Arabia: their past is also different from hers.

Rabia's own negotiations in the third space suggest that she has translated the politics of religious prescription and minority exclusions into a clear, active, and independent articulation of what it means to be a Muslim woman. For her, ambivalence is an existential condition that is dependent on the structural contradictions within the construction of Muslim female identity. While it could be asserted that the structural and emotional contradictions and expressions of ambivalence overlap, Rabia's response indicates a clear distinction between the two. This leads me to identify her expressions of contradiction as structural ambivalence rather than emotional dissonance.

Ayesha

Ayesha is fair-skinned and from an upper-middle-class background. She was born in Egypt in 1949 and lived in the United States from the time she was three until she turned eight in 1957, when her family went back to Egypt. Ayesha went to a private girls' school in Egypt where English was the language of instruction and, she says, the curriculum Western-oriented. She considers herself quite Europeanized and says that the people with whom she moved in Egypt were also of the same class and westernized as well. Upon graduation, she went to the University of Alexandria and received a B.A. in fine arts and in Canada graduated with a B.Ed. from the University of Toronto.

Twenty-two years ago, in 1977, she and her husband and their two children, who were age two and five at the time, immigrated to Canada. They wanted to experience life in North America:

> Ayesha: We came with a round-trip ticket so after a year or two if we decided this is not what we wanted, we would just go back, but we are still here.

In Egypt, Ayesha's sense of herself stemmed from her upper-middle-class status, which placed her within certain social relationships and with resources such as a westernized education. Immigration to Canada disrupted these patterns. Not only was her position of relative privilege affected, but she was also destabilized emotionally and spiritually. Speaking of the importance of Islam in her life she says:

> Ayesha: In Egypt it [Islam] was the norm, and I was the norm. When I came here, I quickly realized it [Islam] was not the norm, and if I wanted my children to grow up with the same type of values that I grew up with . . . praying and fasting, no intoxicants, no pork, the whole package, it would be hard. . . . [Yet] praying brought a great deal of stability to my life.
>
> Shahnaz: The spiritual aspect of Islam was important to you?
>
> Ayesha: Always. . . . There is no doubt when you come to a new country. . . . We started from scratch, from zero, and we had to re-qualify. . . . Whenever it was a difficult time, and even when the weather was bad, . . . we could pray. . . . I am very proud of being a Muslim. It has given me a great deal of peace. Actually it happened in Canada, because I didn't feel that I needed it in Egypt. It was part of my existence in Egypt.

Since Islam was a part of her milieu in Egypt, Ayesha was not particularly invested in authenticity and tradition. Yet like Iram and Rabia, as well as Mussarat, Manal, and Tuzeen (whose experiences I will discuss later), Ayesha lives more consciously as a Muslim woman in Canada. Her faith helped her survive the immigration process and provides stability in her life. Yet being a Muslim also has drawbacks. Particularly at the university she attended in Canada, Ayesha realized that people were responding to her through stereotypes about the authentic and traditional Arab/Muslim woman. Of her university experience she says:

> Ayesha: It was wonderful, I enjoyed it immensely. . . . I gained recognition very quickly. I really enjoyed [the fact] that I was excelling at what I was doing. . . . I think they [her colleagues] were very surprised.
>
> Shahnaz: What response did you get?
>
> Ayesha: In the body language. . . . I never hesitated to chair a committee, for example, or be vocal in any group work that we were doing. . . . I could tell by their body language that they were surprised.

Ayesha's colleagues also had dress expectations of her:

> Ayesha: They asked me, "How come you are dressed like that?" . . . which was normal European clothes, and "Why are you not dressed in your native clothes?" And I said, "Well in the first place not everybody is dressed in black" . . . and I explain to them that there were people [who] because of religion, sometimes prefer to wear the traditional Muslim dress.

Ayesha believes that misinformation causes these stereotypes. Like Iram, she did not hesitate to correct misperceptions whenever she had the chance. (This is also true of Tuzeen, as I will show later.) Ayesha pointed out that her very presence broke every stereotype people had, both at university and where she works. "I think there was a lot of ignorance, they had never personally experienced anyone from Egypt."

The ignorance Ayesha claims she encounters within the dominant culture also marginalizes her. In the Arab/Muslim/Egyptian community she does not feel marginalized. Ayesha has been able to use her westernized education and take advantage of leadership opportunities within the Egyptian community of which she is a part. She has created a seemingly stable space for herself. Her positioning herself as a Muslim has in part allowed her to assume a leadership role made possible through multicultural practices. She has been elected trustee of a heritage language school. Yet within the community she also has to confront issues of authenticity as a Muslim woman that she never had to while she was in Egypt in the mid-seventies.[11]

In particular she has to wrestle with such issues as impositions of the double standard for women and men and *Shari'a*. I do not mean to suggest that only Muslim women have to confront the double standard. Instead, I want to point out that Ayesha, who believes in the equality of women and men, faces contradictions because she also accepts unequal treatment as part of Islam. As she invests in the notion of Muslim woman through multicultural practices, she appears to be embracing rituals that determine her position as unequal with men. At the same time, her narrative suggests a desire to affirm herself as a woman who believes in gender equality and the right to choose.

Ayesha's negotiations of these irresolvable contradictions provide instances of her negotiations in the third space. The contradictions she faces are particularly evident in her interactions with her daughter.

Ayesha: It is very important for me that my daughter grow up with the same values that I grew up with. In order for her to do this in this society, it is going to be a struggle. So I had to explain to her where I was coming from and why I was putting certain restrictions. It is not only where my daughter is concerned; it is my son, too—until they grow to a certain age and it [values] is well embedded in them. The choices that they make hopefully will be the right ones, because I can't be there for them all the time. I am talking about the fact that they are Muslim, that they pray, that they know they are Muslim, that they know what they are going to do.

Shahnaz: What about sexuality?

Ayesha: Where my daughter is concerned, no sex before marriage.

Shahnaz: What about your son?

Ayesha: Same thing, and forget about being a Muslim or not a Muslim. It is a time and age right now [such that] you have to be extremely careful because of everything that is happening health-wise. . . . Now I would be a hypocrite and a liar if I said that my son is as religious in following this as my daughter [is].

Shahnaz: So you have restrictions on both?

Ayesha: Yes, I enforce it on both. On my son, I let up after a while. I am also very realistic.

Shahnaz: Do you find any contradiction in that?

Ayesha: Yes I do. I laugh about it, and my daughter does, too. I explain it to her: "Look, I am not going to give any excuses. I was brought up this way. I didn't turn out too badly. I want the same for you. Please don't say that I am sexist or whatever, because it is very important to me that you are protected until a certain age."

Frigga Haug (1987) argues that through the process of socialization we rationalize and restructure the components of our lives in such a way as to accommodate contradictions. Ayesha has a double standard and recognizes the contradictions. Yet she rationalizes, accepts, and lives these contradictions, particularly those that reinforce conventional choices, without expressing emotional dissonance. Patriarchal community definitions require some aspects of traditionalism from "authentic" women among their members, and these are accepted as authoritative by those who promote multicultural policies.[12] As Nira Yuval-Davis (1994) points out, "community" prescriptions of proper behavior for women distinguish those who belong from those who do not. Through linking her daughter's morality to Islamic identity, Ayesha has made a connection between the community's sense of morality and that which she wants to prescribe to her daughter. Yet Ayesha's connection to traditionalism manifests itself in more ways than through mothering a Muslim daughter. She is connected to the category of Muslim woman within multicultural practices that require her to defend traditionalism more than she would perhaps be likely to on her own if she is to present herself in a leadership role within the "Muslim community."

At times, when Ayesha sees and names inequalities (for example, the double standard for women and men), she accepts them and does not express ambivalence. At other times, particularly around *Shari'a*, it is different.

Shahnaz: What do you think about having *Shari'a* in Canada?

Ayesha: I think it is about time that these things are recognized.

Shahnaz: What is recognized?

Ayesha: The whole concept of Islam. . . .

Shahnaz: Do you think that *Shari'a* will tell people what true Islam is?

Ayesha: Maybe not. . . . It would have to be a choice . . . for those people who feel they are ready for it.

So while Ayesha accepts the importance of *Shari'a* as a way of recognition for Muslims, she realizes that *Shari'a* was probably man-made and not a divine law.

Ayesha: I don't think it [*Shari'a*] is divine. There are a lot of things there that have merit, but there are a lot of things that need to be re-evaluated.

Ayesha reiterated that acceptance of the requirements of *Shari'a* "would have to be a choice."

Shahnaz: But what if it is not a choice? Some situations are structured in such a way that it is not really a choice.

Ayesha: Then I don't think it should be [imposed]. . . . Then it will not fit into the norm of life in Canada.

Shahnaz: Would you choose it?

Ayesha: Myself right now? No probably not, because I don't feel that I am ready for it just yet. Yet I feel that one of the most just and one of the most correct ways of life is the Islamic way of life, and I believe that if most governments followed that [*Shari'a*], we would not have any problems.

I have previously argued (1993) that it is highly unlikely that women would willingly and gladly "choose" to arrange their lives according to laws that give them unequal status. Their "choices" would no doubt be influenced by their sense of the centrality of *Shari'a* in the lives of Muslims, as well as pressure from within their communities and families to conform. Should they decline to be governed by *Shari'a* and find themselves ostracized by their families and their community, they would have to confront the discrimination of the larger Canadian population because they are both women and Muslim, and without community support to fall back on.

Ayesha's response suggests that being willing and being glad are not necessarily the same thing. Although she is not ready for it yet, she seems willing to endorse *Shari'a* in Canada for those who choose it. However, she is not willing to have it imposed on all Muslim women. Her support for it is not enthusiastic, and she is not ready for it herself. She has accepted but does not fundamentally believe in the unequal status of women in *Shari'a*, in particular unequal inheritance stipulations for women.

Ayesha: I am going to tell you [sighs] that I don't believe that a girl should inherit half of what a boy does. . . . And I am saying it, but I feel guilty saying it. . . . It would hurt me to say that I don't agree with it.

In her partial and reluctant acceptance of the double-standard requirements of *Shari'a*, Ayesha's response suggests emotional dissonance as opposed to struggles with standards/power that are consciously unacceptable (as in the cases of Iram, Zubaida, and Safieh).

Ayesha's response revealed to me something about the nature of the complex range of responses to *Shari'a* that I had not acknowledged before.

Ayesha appears to accept the centrality of *Shari'a* as part of the Muslim woman's identity, yet she also disclaims the unfairness. It hurts her to disclaim something she thinks is central and important and divine, because to disavow *Shari'a* is in a sense to disavow her identity. Thus, it hurts her not simply because she will experience external ostracism from the community, but also guilt over what she perceives as her betrayal of Islamic tenets that she believes are mandatory. As Ayesha struggles against the sexist definition of her identity within the community of which she is a part, she also imaginatively negotiates the forums allocated to multicultural minorities within Canada. She rethinks and repositions earlier and current codes of authority as she creates a diasporic space for herself in her new location. In this space spirituality, emotionality, and rationality reconfigure in unique ways to reinforce a Muslim identity from which Ayesha draws strength in Canada.

Karima

Karima, forty-four years old, is white-skinned and originally from Iran. Farsi was the language of instruction at the school that she attended in her small town, and she does not speak English very well. During the interview she spoke mainly in Farsi (with some English), and Safieh, another interviewee, interpreted.

An Arab, Karima was part of a minority in Iran. Her family came to Canada three years ago to escape harassment in Iran during the Iran/Iraq war. She says that she had a good life in Iran, but that the war "messed" everything up. The supermarket attached to their house was bombed, and they had to leave. They moved farther away from the border, but, she recalls, "The war kept following us." Then her husband lost his job. He is an Arab and was therefore suspected of opposing the Iranian revolution. Although her sisters finished school and went on to become teachers, Karima did not graduate; instead, at seventeen, she married her brother-in-law's brother. Karima did not go to college, and she connects lack of education with lack of power and mobility for women.

Karima and her husband did not know any English when they came to Canada, and they could not find work. At one point they did not go out of the house for six months. Her husband was always nervous and angry, and both of them cried a lot.

> Karima: We thought, "Why did we come out to Canada? Now we don't have anything. Back home at least we had the family." . . . Somebody stole our money, too. We couldn't go back to Iran either. . . . My husband

was angry at me . . . because he had all the problems in life, and the only person who was a punching box was me. He wasn't a person who would beat me up, but like verbally. . . .

Karima worked as a beautician in Iran. In Canada she works as a cook/ waitress in a restaurant she and her husband run but do not own.

To an extent Karima's narrative draws upon the notion of the Muslim collective the *Umma,* and her life in Canada appears polarized with her conceptualization of a utopian past in Iran under Khomeini. Yet the concept of a cohesive Muslim collective can be quite fragile, for indeed the unity of the mythical *Umma* could not prevent the Iran/Iraq war. In this conflict between two Muslim countries she and her husband as Arab minorities in Iran were considered undesirable and came to Canada as refugees.

Karima: They were saying that he [her husband] helped Saddam. I lost everything and only got the children out. They didn't have shoes on even. . . . All the family lived in relatives' houses. Everybody lost everything, so I can't even go back to stay with somebody else. . . . I was upset because they were Muslim, too, and that these two powers, Khomeini and Saddam, are creating everything. It [was] not the people.

In this narrative of diasporic displacement, Karima factors in the myth of solidarity of the Muslim collective by blaming the leaders of the two countries and pointing out that they, not the people, were responsible for war. In this way she was able to integrate war between Muslim countries into her utopian vision of her past life in Iran.

Karima asserts that she had a good life in Iran, until the war with Iraq destroyed it.

Shahnaz: What was it like living in Iran under Khomeini?

Karima: I loved it for not having drinks, like alcohol. . . . In Shah's time they [men] would go out and drink, and they would come home late at night and become abusive. . . . And I liked it [living under the Khomeini regime] for the cover-up, . . . the *hejab,* because it is comfortable and gives *rahat* [peace].

Karima's identity in Iran was enacted in her everyday negotiations and involved her family and social networks. This provided her with a stable space and a certain degree of empowerment. These were disrupted when the Iran/Iraq war brought to the fore her minority status as an Arab in Iran. Amrita Chhachhi (1989) argues that romanticized "traditionalism" is often precipitated by the disintegration of familial and kinship structures. Karima's extended family networks have either disintegrated due to war or have been left behind in Iran. Her memories of her life in Iran appear to be crucial in maintaining a continuity with her identity as a Muslim woman.

As Karima cannot replicate her networks in Canada, her identity as a Muslim woman becomes more dependent on the enactment of practices that provide her with a sense of continuity of self as a Muslim woman. Yet Karima's notions of the authentic Muslim woman's everyday enactments conflict with the mechanics of her actual life in Canada. For instance, she does not believe that Muslims should drink, yet in Canada she is placed in the position of selling alcohol in her restaurant.

> Karima: In the restaurant we are full of sins. At the beginning when I was working here, [if] somebody wanted something from the bar, I would tell them that I don't work for the bar, I work for the restaurant, I am in this section, not that section. Somebody else would get it. Back home [in Iran] my husband would drink sometimes, and [if] anything bad happens [*sic*] in the house, I would tell him that it was because of the drinking.

Karima regards nonconsumption as central for Muslim women. In selling liquor she compromises herself. However, in her case the compromise is born not out of a need to create cultural meaning and pleasure, but out of material necessity. The ambivalence she expresses is muted and comes out of a need to have a Muslim identity and her difficulty in fully enacting it in Canada.

Karima also faces contradictions because she believes *Shari'a* is "Islam's law" and that the Muslim woman must adhere to it. At the same time, she does not think Islamic inheritance laws are fair. Her father did not leave a will, and she got only half as much as her brothers. Moreover, Karima believes that if *Shari'a* is used to oppress a woman, then she should reject it and even Islam itself:

> Karima: She should say, "I am not a Muslim," . . . so the law would not apply to her.
>
> Shahnaz: What do you think will happen to that woman in terms of heaven and hell?
>
> Karima: She will go to hell. . . .
>
> Shahnaz: If the woman has to say that she is not a Muslim in order to survive in this society, wouldn't God understand and accept the problem as it is and not send her to hell?
>
> Karima: Maybe God understands because I don't know what God does. Maybe God understands, and she wouldn't go to hell. If the woman

says that she is not a Muslim, and she has to say that, God may forgive her because of the good things that she does.

Karima says that she would sympathize with a woman put in the position of disavowing Islam in order to survive: "I will not judge; God will judge." Even though she is not ready to submit to the oppressive nature of Islamic law, her narrative reinforces being and doing Muslim through belief in God and community action.

Karima recognizes that in Canada she often engages in practices that differ from the daily rituals with which she is familiar. Yet she never denies the validity of those familiar practices. She hopes that God will decide in her favor, and she wrestles with the notion of being more observant than she is. She expresses ambivalence about some of her practices that are not in keeping with the familiar Muslim requirements for women. She is clear about her identity as a Muslim, but she can succeed in Canada materially, socially, and psychologically only to the degree she fails as a Muslim. This paradox is painful for Karima.

The mothering of the next generation of Muslims, particularly females, is a crucial issue for the Muslim woman. Karima tries to extend everyday practices of her Muslim identity to her daughters, but she faces opposition:

Karima: They [the girls] don't know what is good for them.

Shahnaz: What is good for them?

Karima: A girl is supposed to be a girl to all the points in Islam, and God and the Prophet have said they have to go along with that. They have to listen to the parents.

Shahnaz: But in every Muslim household there are different points that the parents stress. What points do you stress?

Karima: I want my daughters to be the girlish type. When they are living under my roof, I want them to cover themselves, not the head, but the body. They can't wear short skirts, always long. . . . I don't mind if they don't pray and they don't fast. It is the dress code, the going out, no boyfriends, no sex before marriage. They have to stay a virgin till the day they get married. . . . They can't go around like a man.

Karima's story suggests cultural affirmations through prescriptions of morality for women, an attempt to keep women chaste and pure and firmly within the collective. For Karima more than any of the women interviewed, the Muslim woman's identity appears to be reduced to control of the girl children without accompanying spiritual or ritualized requirements.

Karima endorses the control of her daughters, which is enforced primarily by her sons, and also by her husband.

> Karima: Like ten minutes late, if they come back, they are going to get into trouble, because you know, they [brothers] want an account for every minute. The elder brother, he is twenty-three. He is more strict even than the father. He comes home and tells the fourteen year old that he does not like the "false nail you have on." The girl doesn't say anything because he is standing there and he is mad, but [later] she tells me "What does he want from me? He has a girlfriend himself." And I say, "Men have needs. . . . The girls have to get married. They can't go around like a man."
>
> Shahnaz: Do your daughters listen to you?
>
> Karima: They get upset, but I don't listen to them.
>
> Shahnaz: What do they say?
>
> Karima: They are kids. They don't listen. I tell them we are Muslim. They get upset, [and] they say "Oh, well, I don't want to be Muslim if you are going to control me so much." They don't understand.

The category of Muslim that is mobilized by Karima's family focuses on the social and sexual control of the girl child and on the role of the Muslim mother in maintaining it. However, control of the Muslim woman (which prescriptions of Islamist authenticity demand) comes in conflict with economics. As more and more women find themselves working outside the home for money, conventional methods of controlling women, such as seclusion, are no longer an option. Although Karima herself worked outside the home in Iran, she was in an environment where familial and societal pressures reinforced control of the women. Here in Canada these controls are challenged not only by society but by her daughters as well.

Outside influences nothwithstanding, Karima is aware that her daughters cannot be secluded; they need education for employment. And she claims that her own life would have been different if she had had more education.

> Karima: If I had studied, I would have become somebody. I don't have that much status. If I had studied I wouldn't have needed a translator. I would have been able to talk. If I had studied, I would have been able to drive a car. In Iran I had everything economically, but because I did not study, my education was very limited. I want my daughters to have more education. I want her [sic] to become a doctor or somebody so that she has status.

She cites better education and employment prospects for her daughters in Canada as another reason for leaving Iran. In sending them to school, Karima hopes that her daughters will become physicians and, as such, valued members of Canadian society—something she with little status lacks. However, she has grave concerns about the freedoms her daughters will be exposed to in school, which she will not be able to control:

> Karima: In the class, the girls are sitting here, the boys are sitting here. They are watching sex education classes and anatomy, and that is not right. . . . And my son sees the condom commercial, and he says, "What is that?" I say "It is not for you." If the children go and ask the teacher, she says, "That is [a] condom." If they ask in Iran, the teacher would say, "When you grow up, you will know," rather than explain it to him.

Condoms are perceived as useless for children because Karima does not believe that the children from Iran and other Muslim countries engage in sexual relations. As Yasmin Ali (1992) points out, within the discourse of "the community," an ahistorical and romanticized view of the 'old country' is presented within the transplanted community in the First World. This view contains edited versions of "home" that are more in harmony with the ideal than with the complexity of current practices and that date back to the period when members of diasporic communities left their home countries. Life has changed in their countries of origin, but their nostalgic views remain frozen in time. Such edited and nostalgic views deny the sexuality of Karima's teenage daughters.

While Karima voices concerns over her ability to exercise control over her daughters in Canada, she is aware of the opportunities they have here.

> Karima: I am afraid of the effect of things here on the children. The drinking and dancing . . . the sleeveless dress. I am afraid of too much freedom for the girls. [Otherwise] education is good, and everything is good. The children can study without having much money, and if we were in Iran, we would have to send them out here and we would have paid a lot of money for them to study here. It is great [in Canada], but all the prostitution and all the openness, all the sexual freedom, I don't like.

Karima's life in Canada is such that she is not always able to enact her vision of herself as a Muslim woman or the Muslim mother anymore than she can enforce her ideals for her daughters.

> Karima: Everybody goes to hell anyway [laughs] because we don't cover up, because we don't do fasting. So what the heck, you know, we sell alcohol here. We have done it ourself [sic] in our restaurant.

Shahnaz: So you don't believe in drinking alcohol, but you sell it anyway?

Karima: I have to sell it because our life depends on selling things. And I can't cover up because I am serving in a restaurant.

As a woman who believes that particular practices delineate a Muslim identity, being able to enact those practices matters to Karima. The ways of serving God are prescribed, and if one does not follow the prescriptions in this world, one will not be rewarded in the next. Her statement "what the heck" suggests that she is feeling trapped in circumstances she cannot control. Thus it doesn't matter if she sells alcohol because of all the other sins that she has committed. As she says "what the heck," she comes close to disavowing something that is fundamental to her notion of Muslim identity.

Karima's past life in Iran is central to her notion of identity and culture in Canada. This past is part of the myth of the beyond, within which, Bhabha argues, individuals often locate culture. Yet, "the 'beyond' is neither a new horizon, nor a leaving behind of the past . . . [instead] we find ourselves in the moment of transit where space and time cross to produce complex figures of difference and identity, past and present, inside and outside, inclusion and exclusion" (1994a, 1). In Bhabha's notion of culture there is no past and future; culture is always constructed in the present moment. Although Karima's erasure of the difficulties she experienced in her homeland helps to polarize her view of her world—Iran versus Canada—her story conveys how she constructs her culture in Canada in the present. She negotiates in the third space, even as that negotiation draws on her life in Iran and purist notions of female identity. It could be that she reconciles herself to Canada, not just out of material necessity but because of a recognition that the homeland society and her life in that society were already riddled with tension and contradictions. Her comment "what the heck" suggests that her notion of self as Muslim woman and Muslim mother is unworkable in Canada. Karima comes close to questioning the overall structure of Muslim womanhood and to regarding the everyday practices central to her notion of identity as an impossibility in her current life. And yet because of a notion of identity that focuses on the past she cannot have, her logic leads her to conclude that she is damned to hell.

Mussarat (Iram's mother)

Mussarat is brown-skinned. Originally from India, Mussarat's family had been living in Zaire for four generations. When she was eighteen, she married a twenty-two-year-old Muslim of Indian origin whose family had settled in Uganda. Mussarat went to a missionary school in what was then the Belgian Congo (now Zaire) where she learned French.

She had not married the young man that she was in love with "because he was drinking, and that was forbidden, right?" Her family chose the man she married. She had seen him just once.

Mussarat: I never had the chance to talk [to him]. I had just seen [him]. I went to [sic] my vacation, and all of a sudden somebody tells me that this guy is going to ask you for marrying [sic] him. And I said that I have not seen him that way. I have just had a glance at him, and that is it. I mean that is not enough.

Shahnaz: What was the basis of your parents' choosing him for you do you think?

Mussarat: He is standing on his own two feet, and he has the money. He is from a good family, like khandan [family]. They said to me, "You know he has [the] education, and . . . [we] don't think that you will be unhappy. What more would you look for in men than you have got already [in him]?" I did not have much to say when I got engaged, and I had . . . second thought[s] and tried to get out of [it], but I could not.

Mussarat and her husband and children came to Canada in 1971 when she was twenty-six and the youngest of her three daughters was two months old. Her husband wanted a son.

Mussarat: The first two daughters were welcome, you know. The third one was the time when he really got angry. He was expecting me to have a son, which I wanted too, but if I cannot have a son, what am I going to do? It is not up to me. One friend of mine, she came to say, "Congratulations, Mussarat." And I said, "You must be thinking that I wanted a son, and I did not get one. But I love my daughter very dearly. Third one, right?" And right away my ex-husband told her that "Why don't you take her away, because we have the machine to produce daughters here anyway." Right in front of her. So we just looked at each other, and I had tears in my eyes [starts crying]. And that is it.

Because she did not produce a son, Mussarat's husband, who had a violent temper, physically and emotionally abused her throughout their twenty-two-year marriage. She did not tell her family of this abuse because she said "It would have hurt them." Other people, however, told her family of the abuse. They suggested that Mussarat leave her husband, but she decided against it:

> Mussarat: For a Muslim, it says that a daughter from a good upbringing [*sic*] family should not leave. . . .
>
> Shahnaz: Where does it say that?
>
> Mussarat: The *khandan*.
>
> Shahnaz: The *Qur'an*?
>
> Mussarat: No, in the *Qur'an* it does not say [that], but the family, the customs, that a daughter from a good family . . .

Mussarat went on to reiterate that women from good families do not leave their husbands, although she knew that it was allowed in Islam. She decided to make her marriage work somehow, although she is aware that her former husband never tried to make it work. The marriage did not last, however. Mussarat finally left him because her daughters talked her into it. She was forty-seven years old at the time of the interview and has been on her own since 1985.

Mussarat's story suggests that she is invested in the notion of Muslim female identity in Canada much more than she ever was growing up in Zaire. Religion is one of her main supports:

> Shahnaz: Did being a Muslim make a difference to you . . . in Zaire?
>
> Mussarat: At that time, no, because we did not know exactly what the religion said. . . . But coming to this country, we are finding out more and more stuff.
>
> Shahnaz: Tell me the difference about then and now, about there and here.
>
> Mussarat: [In Zaire] now young little girls, nine years old, as soon as they start puberty, they start wearing the veil.
>
> Shahnaz: What was it like when you were growing up?
>
> Mussarat: Oh, I wore shorts and "minis." It was not a big deal being Muslim. It was part of society.

In Canada it was different: "He [God] has helped me through hell, and I believe in him more and more." Mussarat's faith helped her spiritually at a time when the immigration process had disrupted her family network, and an abusive marriage further intensified the isolation she felt. This isolation was exacerbated by her lack of proficiency in English. She was fluent in French, but this did not help Mussarat in Vancouver where she, along with her husband and daughters, spent the first two months living in a motel. Not only did he not help her face adjustment issues, he did not speak to her at all. In spite of her unfamiliarity with the system and language, she recalls that he expected her to carry on the household chores as usual.

> Mussarat: First of all having three children on my own—my youngest one . . . was only five months old, and she was teething, and every tooth that she would get, she would have a fever for three weeks. I did not know my way. I did not know what to do. I had to cook proper meals, like chapattis, curry, and rice, every day. And on top of that, instead of helping me, he would bring some other people to come and have dinner with me. So one day I got so mad I said "I am not your maid. I am so busy looking after the children. I have to cook. I mean how much am I going to do? These people, they are such a young couple they have got nothing to do, and they come here and have supper every day." And we were living on the money of the government that they used to give us, thirty-two dollars a week.

> Shahnaz: And he was expecting you to provide food with that.

> Mussarat: Oh, yes.

> Shahnaz: And to go shopping, too, and bring groceries.

> Mussarat: My seven-year-old daughter, when she would come to the motel for lunch, I would tell her to look after her sisters for half an hour, and I would just go to the corner to get some meat and eggs, and whatever I needed. . . . And he did not talk to me all those two months . . . for no reason. I did not know how to use the washing machine, so I told him, "How am I going to do the washing machine?" He said, "Why don't you take it to laundromat and ask somebody?" At that time I did not know English. Now who am I going to ask? There are all white people doing laundry. And on the top of it I was so embarrassed to go and ask how to do the laundry, because first of all the language barrier, second, people would think "What kind of, you know, uncivilized people have come in here who don't know how to use a washing machine?" I had never seen a washing machine before. So I had to do it with my hands in my bathroom. And within a couple of months I had rashes in all my arms and hands.

Her experiences illustrate the pain and suffering she endured when she arrived in Canada. Yet her experiences also testify to her embracing the importance of being in a marriage and accepting abuse, based on the assumption that she must do so as a woman from a good Muslim family.

A key aspect of Mussarat's notion of Muslim womanhood is the concept of marriage. Fatna Sabah has pointed out that the institution of marriage is part of the sacred construction of reality in Islam, a reality, she argues, that is constructed through a power relationship between the sacred and the sexual: "In the Muslim universe there is no purely sexual field, there is only a regulated sexual field, coded and systemized according to the options and priorities of Islam as a culture and a strategy for civilization" (1984, 65).

A single woman's sexuality can cause *fitna* (social chaos), and so must be regulated within the domestic sphere. As such Mussarat's sexuality needs to be contained. Mussarat has accepted such messages:

> Mussarat: In Muslim religion it is forbidden to stay alone, because your heart will desire to go everywhere else, you know, and that is totally forbidden. So that is why the religion encourages you to go and find yourself a suitable person and get married as soon as possible. . . . But you don't have to put up with anybody's "bullshit." God does not like very much the divorces, but at the same time, he does not ask you to stay with the person that does not love you.

Despite her belief that Muslim women are allowed to divorce husbands who do not love them, Mussarat stayed in an abusive marriage for twenty-two years. As such, she accepted the notion of a good woman who stays in a marriage, even an abusive one, and tried to make it work.

Mussarat identifies with the category of Muslim woman and attempts to resolve some of the structural contradictions. After twenty-two years of confronting and enacting the Muslim woman's role in an abusive marriage, she finally left the marriage only to find that the contradictions were not easily resolved. She continues to confront the Muslim woman identity at work where she is often teased by her coworkers.

> Shahnaz: So how do you feel being a Muslim woman in this country?
>
> Mussarat: Being a Muslim, I got teased quite a bit in my work because I am the only Muslim woman working there. . . . They [her coworkers] say, "Mussarat, wear your veil now. We want you to be like other Muslim women." They said, "You should be walking behind us." I said, "Forget it." One guy asked me whether I am the "good Muslim" or the "bad Muslim." He was serious about this question, and I did not understand. I said, "What is a good Muslim, and what is a bad Muslim?" He said, "The good Muslim are the people who believe in Aga Khan, and the bad Muslims are the ones who believe in Khomeini." I said, "Sorry, I am the bad Muslim."
>
> Shahnaz: What did he say?
>
> Mussarat: Oh, he just laughed as if he was embarrassed and said, "Sorry, I didn't mean it that way." I said, "I am not sorry. It is a good

thing that you asked." I still tell them all if they tease me. I say, "Hey, I am proud to be a Muslim."

Her pride in being a Muslim is part of a series of contradictions in her life. Mussarat finds that the Muslim woman has restrictions on her sexuality, but she is lonely and wants to have a relationship with a man. After living in an extremely violent marriage, Mussarat is not sure she wants to get married. She thinks that Muslim men would find her too independent, and she wants to date white men whom she considers less sexist. Her "modern" colonial-style education at a missionary school as well as the Orientalist assumptions of the society where she lives might have reinforced the colonial rhetoric that "Other" men are more oppressive than Euro-American men. She claims: "I will never find a Muslim guy for myself. They are too demanding—they are too narrow minded. And I am too much Canadianized." Mussarat's story suggests that colonial education, Islamic patriarchal culture, her early immigration experience, and violence from her husband intersect in interesting ways, so much so that she refuses the powerlessness of the Muslim woman's position by rejecting Muslim men. Yet Mussarat does not totally refuse the position of Muslim woman. She has accepted being sexually active only through *muta* and to an extent ideas of embodiment and dress.[13]

As a Shia Muslim, Mussarat has the choice of contracting a *muta* marriage. However, this choice causes a dilemma for her. Referring to Muslim and Canadian men as mutually exclusive groups, she says she is "too Canadianized to date a Muslim man" and expects that "Canadian" men will want to have sex with her, which is permitted her as an unmarried Shia woman within the institution of *muta*. She periodically goes to a woman preacher for advice and guidance regarding *muta*. From what the preacher said, Mussarat realized that *muta* was sexist:

> Mussarat: I never had the time to read it [the *Qur'an*], so I really don't know much, but I do know the basics. If I want to go and have sex with somebody, it has to be a Muslim man, and I have to make him sign a contract for a hour or two or whatever, *muta*.
>
> Shahnaz: What about men?
>
> Mussarat: They are abusing the system: they should do the *muta* as well. But I learned from this lady preacher that . . . a Muslim guy is allowed to do *muta* with a non-Muslim girl, but I can't do *muta* with a non-Muslim guy. I [loudly] I gave her such a big lecture. I said "I thought God said we are all equal. What happened?"

Mussarat learned that as a woman, she could only do *nikah* (permanent marriage) or *muta* with a Muslim man. She believes that if she asks a man to become a Muslim to marry her (permanent or temporary), he will say "forget it." Mussarat does not fully accept or embrace prescriptions from the preacher for the Muslim woman. She is beginning to reject what she terms "bullshit" and is not sure for how long she will be able to absorb the sexism.

Mussarat confronts rigid sexist codes of authority about *muta* and disclaims them. But she never disavows her Muslimness. She continues to find spiritual strength in Islam and is confident that her everyday practices are that of a Muslim, though not without contradictions. In particular she faces contradictions around notions of embodiment and dress. She accepts the prescriptions to a certain extent but does not always subscribe to them. For instance, she wears shorts, although she believes doing so goes against the modesty requirements of Islam. As for the future she would like to see changes:

Mussarat: That we [women and men] all have the same rights. . . . [Also,] I can do anything that I feel—like I am not allowed to wear pants, and I am doing it anyway. You know I am not covering myself the way a Muslim should be covering. . . . As far as I know, if your heart is clean, if those men stare at you the way I get stared at wherever I go, that is their problem, not mine.

The advice Mussarat receives from the preacher also contains prescriptions about the *hejab* and dating.

Shahnaz: Do you feel restrained by what the preacher tells you?

Mussarat: I do. I haven't been with a man in the last five years. If I am not allowed to date, how am I going to be with a man? . . . It makes me really angry. It makes me angry being a Muslim woman, too. . . . I am caught between two . . . between Muslim and Canadian society, and I would love to go for a date. People ask me to go out . . . but I cannot because it is *haram* [forbidden]. It is *haram* to go out with a man for a date. I have to wear my veil, and I never wear a veil. It is in the back of my mind, but I still do not have the courage to do it. And I don't think that if I wear a veil anybody is going to ask me to go out.

Mussarat appears caught in the discontinuous time of translation and negotiation in the third space. Despite her realization that being a Muslim may not be workable for her both in dress and sexual activity, Mussarat continues to invest in being a Muslim woman. She is angry for imposing barriers on herself for many years and staying in an abusive relationship. Now that she is no longer in that relationship, she feels that the barriers still exist, although she is not sure for how much longer. So far she has allowed the preacher's interpretations to control her sexuality.

Mussarat's investment in a Muslim identity, although unsure and at times unworkable, is also necessary, as it provides a spiritual component to her life. Her spiritual beliefs sustained her through the trauma of abuse and isolation she went through in Canada.

Mussarat: I do respect, honestly from the bottom of my heart, my religion, because God has really helped me all these years.

Mussarat's talk indicates that accepting herself as a Muslim woman also means embracing a notion of herself about which she has ambivalent feelings. Moreover, Mussarat tries to extend this notion (particularly the restrictions on sexual activity) to her daughters.

Mussarat: It bothers me when my children go "clubbing" and dancing and all that.

Shahnaz: What bothers you?

Mussarat: Because if I can do without it [sex] for five years . . . I am still young—I am in the peak of my time. I thought that I had raised you guys right, you know, sex is only with one man, your husband. . . . But they don't believe in that. They say "Mom, that has changed. You are not in the same country that you grew up in." I tell them my story, [and] they say, "Mom, we don't want to hear your story. We have heard enough."

Shahnaz: How does that make you feel?

Mussarat: It makes me angry. . . . I tell them, "Go to hell. All of you go to hell. Leave me alone, because now I have given up."

Mussarat's story suggests that she has mixed feelings about many requirements of Islamic practice, yet she feels the pressure of having to be responsible for the sexuality / morality of her daughters. She believes it is her duty as a Muslim mother to instruct her daughters regarding the correct path for a Muslim woman. Her daughters, however, do not see it that way. They have made it quite clear that times have changed, and they are not interested in restrictions. Mussarat appears to be torn concerning the issue of sexuality. She has expressed an interest in being involved with someone but cannot because of her own internalized constraints. Yet, she is particularly disturbed that her children's actions conflict with her notions of the ideal Muslim woman's sexuality.

Mussarat embraces yet is angered by the notion of the Muslim woman. On one hand, she is torn between restructuring herself within Islamist and Orientalist notions of Muslim identity. She finds that she cannot accept either fully. On the other hand, her investment in Islamist notions of the Muslim woman for herself and her daughters has remained constant, despite her questioning and at times disregarding the sexist interpretations of religion she receives from the preacher. She sees no immediate resolution for her ambivalence and expresses uncertainty about the future.

> Mussarat: She [preacher] said, "That is the way it is." I said, "I don't know for how long I can absorb this bullshit." I mean you live only once. Why waste your life away by living in rules? . . . Sometimes I think I am wasting my life away.

Her talk indicates that her adherence to traditional notions of Muslim womanhood are not fixed for herself. And this might be part of the reason why she gives up imposing it on her daughters. She challenges the codes and signifiers and, as Anzaldua (1987) would say, turns them into the strength of a mestiza. Yet her pain and indecision indicate that to some extent, she is still mired in the contradictions she negotiates in the third space. In this space, her hybridized subjectivity is marked by shifting cultural and psychic boundaries. Her myths of home and authenticity intersect with her current needs and desires. Both home and location determine her Muslimness as she translates and negotiates her life.

Zahra

Zahra was born in 1967 in Ethiopia to a Somali mother and an Ethiopian father. When she was five, her father died and her mother brought the family back to Somalia. Soon after, she married a Somali man. War and fragmentation of Somali society led Zahra to Canada in 1989 as a refugee.

While in Somalia, Zahra's cultural socialization was in dissonance with what was taught at the first school she attended in Mogadishu, where the language of instruction was Italian, the colonizer's language. In this school the focus was not the Somali culture (Somalia is predominantly Muslim) but Christianity.

> Zahra: . . . And they take you to the church and pray there on Sunday. My stepfather is [sic] really mad one day when I was late, and he said, "What happened to you?" and I said that "We went to church," and he said, "What are you doing there?" And I said that my teacher took me there, and everybody was going there to pray. And he asked me What did I say when I was praying? I told him, I remember, "Son of God which was Jesus Christ, and Maria his mom was carrying this child in the picture, and everybody was staring at it and putting their hands

together and pray [sic] for her." Which at that time I believed it is going to be helpful, and she is going to hear what I say, that is what my teacher told me. It was really so bad because I was a child and I didn't know. My stepfather he say, "No, you aren't going to that school any more. I will apply to another school for you." I said, "No, I don't want to lose my friends." He said, "No, you have to do what I say." And I was really sad. I left that school and went to another school where everything was in Somali language and Arabic as second language. They had Egyptian teachers . . . and they were teaching me things I know, things I learned from home, and things I learned from society.

Shahnaz: Did you like this second school?

Zahra: The other school was making me confused. Because one day . . . I asked my mom, "Why they have this Jesus Christ picture with this woman called Maria?" And she says, "She is just like a doll. Do you believe she can hear you?" So she said, "Why you want to go to that [Italian language] school?" I said, "I understand now." My stepfather was just demanding, my mother try [sic] to explain to me why she doesn't want me to go to that school.

Zahra claims that the Italian school confused her. Meanwhile, in the Somali school she got cultural messages with which she was familiar. These messages, particularly those that focused on a chaste embodied morality for women, were reinforced by her mother.

Zahra: The important thing she used to tell me, "Even if you open [unveil] your hair and do what you want to, don't forget there is one God. Don't forget there is one Prophet Mohammed. And don't forget to cover, to protect, not to do any *haram*." I don't know what they say in English, have body contact with somebody else you are not married to. And she said, "Even if I don't see you, God will see you and God will be with you everywhere."

Zahra appears to have accepted these messages about control of her sexuality:

Zahra: I believe that God will be with me everywhere, so I don't have to just pretend when I am with my Mom and act like a good child. But when I am with myself, I believe it myself.

War and civil disruption in Somalia forced Zahra to go to Italy. She lived there for two and a half years before she was granted status as a refugee in Canada. Zahra's circumstances of civil war in Somalia and refugee status in Italy and Canada disrupted her environment significantly. And these internalized messages of religion and cultural morality have proved to be a significant stable marker in her diasporic dislocation.

Although Zahra is currently a Canadian citizen, she speaks of her very negative experience with Canadian officials. When she was in Italy, she was told by Canadian officials that as a refugee the Canadian government would sponsor her for a year. During this period she could study English and get a high school diploma. (She had completed high school in Somalia, but this was not recognized in Canada.) After she had been here for two months, the immigration counselor called her in. As Zahra did not understand English very well, she took another Somali woman as a translator. The counselor said he had a job for her doing factory work. Failure to take this job would mean loss of government support, he told her. Zahra wanted to study English and continue her education at the university, and she refused the job. The immigration counselor called her a "bitch," she says, " . . . in front of my friend, and he screamed even." Zahra couldn't speak English well enough to answer him back, and because of her experience with government people in Somalia she feared he might have her arrested.

> Zahra: I was afraid the way he talked to me. I thought he would arrest me because I don't have no [sic] family, no one in Canada. They [government officials] knew, when I filled the application in Italy, I don't have . . . friends in Canada. I don't know no [sic] one.

The counselor cut off her benefits. She was without money for five months, living with various friends. Then someone told her she could apply for welfare. She was on welfare until she found work. Because she is good at math, she took computer courses at a community college. Her intention was to work in a bank. Later she found that this course would not give her the skills to get employment at a bank.

In Italy, she had worked with refugees, and one day on the Toronto subway she was approached by three Somali refugee women who were staying at a shelter and who wanted her help. At this point Zahra was trying to figure out which career path to take and thought maybe she should work in a shelter. She applied to a shelter and began to work there.

Zahra's investment in the maintenance of a Muslim identity in Canada stems from the cultural, social, and economic disruptions she faced as a refugee from war-torn Somalia. As she enacts her Muslim identity in Canada, she confronts the categorization of Muslim women in two main spheres of life: her own sexuality and her work at a shelter for women.

In particular her sexuality presents contradictions for Zahra.

> Zahra: When I was in Italy, I never had sex. . . . I was a virgin. . . . I changed when I came to Canada.

> Shahnaz: Why did you change?

Zahra: Because the society was really so stressful, and you needed somebody, some sexual relationship. . . . So it comes from the dark side . . . because Islam says you don't need to have sex before you marry, or if you don't marry, you don't need to be having sex. . . . So now I feel less *iman,* what they call in English faith, because I did these things which I wasn't supposed to do, but I ask God to forgive me.

Shahnaz: Do you feel it was wrong?

Zahra: Yes, totally. I am too shameful. I am not sure what sense it makes for me to have sex for my frustration.

In Canada, Zahra is positioned as black. And as bell hooks (1993) and other theorists have noted, there is an exaggerated emphasis in North America on black women's sexuality. Black women are categorized as hypersexual and available. Zahra appears to have been confronted with the racial stereotypes of black women as extremely sexual. This came into conflict with constraints on her sexuality that Zahra learned through her upbringing in Somalia. She is living this contradiction and has not been able to reconcile the two. She is sexually active outside of marriage, which she believes is forbidden to her as a Muslim. She feels extremely guilty about being so.

Zahra is looking for understanding, and she does not get it from most of the people she meets in Canada. Instead she is confronted by stereotypes about the "black woman" and the Muslim woman. She is also looking for guidance and support in the Somali community, which she does not get either. Instead she learns new ways to be a "better" Muslim woman in Canada.

Zahra: I realize that women go to the masjid [mosque], [but it] doesn't provide for them any program. All they provide there is the religion. That is it, and they tell them how to use the religion, and the rules of the religion which women of Islam have to follow. But they don't realize that there is [sic] a lot of women who have a problem with husband and with children and don't have any place to go with that.

Shahnaz: So you are saying the mosque provides you with the rules of Islam, but not how to do day-to-day living in Canada?

Zahra: Actually I was the one in the community of Somalians who addressed this issue, when women get beat up by husbands. We are Islamic. We are not against Islam, but Muslim religion doesn't say that women have to get beat up. . . . And also that is something to do with the society . . . in Canada. . . . They [non-Muslims] watch all the people which are talking about how it is too bad this culture [Muslim], this tradition devised by this religion [Islam], which they make look bad. I am Muslim; I am not wrong. I believe that I can do whatever I want. I believe I am not a victim for a man. I am not a housekeeper. I can do everything I want. I can go out. I can do marriage and be a good Muslim woman. I don't know if the masjid even realizes [*sic*] the system and society in Canada we live with.

It is ironic, she points out, that in Somalia the dictator Siyad Barre backed progressive legislation on violence against women. He passed a law requiring a ten-year jail sentence for a man who beats his wife. Yet in Canada, Somali women get little support when they face violent partners. At the mosques they are told that if everyone follows Islam, there will be no violence. When they do face violence and seek refuge in a shelter, Zahra claims they face discrimination and harassment.

Most of the residents at the shelter where Zahra worked were Muslim women from Pakistan, Bangladesh, and Iran. She realized that there was no one to attend to their concerns and needs, and that they were too afraid to ask the staff for help. This is because the staff, which consisted of white women and some women of color, had made it quite clear that they disapproved of Islam. There were even greater problems in the month of Ramadan for women. Even though they were fasting all day, they had to leave the shelter in the morning and come back at 5:00 P.M.. Zahra spoke up. Although the management agreed to allow the women to rest in the shelter in the afternoons when they were fasting, they were not willing to provide *halal* meat.[14]

> Zahra: There was an Iranian woman, and she was a Muslim and a client, and her husband was following her. She said, "I can't go out. I am too afraid. I am afraid to step outside." They say . . . "Why don't you call the police." And she wasn't in a position to call the police . . . because she was a very cultural woman, very traditional Islamic woman wearing the *hejab*. She is not going to do that, and she is [*sic*] not growing up in this society. . . . And they couldn't understand. . . . The staff said, "Call the police. This is a free country. You don't have to be afraid. Otherwise we are going to transfer you to another hostel. You have to leave." . . . The woman refused to go or call the police, and she refused to make decisions so quick. So I say, "I am also [an] Islamic woman. Tell me what you want to do." She says, "I want to call my uncle." [That was] her solution, which I understand . . . because we have the same culture. And the women were saying at the hostel, "Isn't it something ridiculous?" And I say, "What do you mean?" "The religion," they say.

The staff denied Zahra any credibility, refusing to believe that she could be sensitive to the needs of the Muslim women at the shelter.

Zahra: They say, "You are not really Muslim, Zahra. We know you. You don't wear *hejab*. You go with boyfriends or girlfriends and all that stuff." I say, "It has nothing to do with what I believe as a religion. If I cover my hair or if I enjoy with you guys, [it] doesn't mean I am not a Muslim." I really had a hard time because I didn't know what to do.

Orientalist and Islamist determinations of the Muslim woman come with prescribed forms of behavior. Because Zahra, unlike many of the other residents, did not wear the *hejab*, did not adhere to prescriptions such as fasting, prayers, and dietary requirements, and was sexually active outside of marriage, she was placed in the position of not being "Muslim enough." Zahra has partially accepted these prescriptions and feels guilty and less *iman* (faith) because she does not always follow what she believes as a Muslim. Such contradictions leave her at times feeling immobilized.

Zahra's contradictions are compounded by racist understanding of Muslim women at her workplace. Zahra argues that in their attempts to raise women's consciousness, they misguidedly pointed to Islam's oppression of women. The staff at the shelter told Muslim residents who were fasting:

Zahra: "You don't eat all day long. That is sick." This is not good words to say . . . to somebody who believes something, and especially somebody who has come there for shelter.

Moreover, as Ahmed (1982) argues, Muslim women are often seen as backward, passive, and oppressed by religion, and as objects to be liberated from Muslim men. Zahra was told by her coworkers that she should be grateful that she was in Canada and did not have to put up with Islamic oppression:

Zahra: "Muslim women are slaves, being at home and cooking for men. Did you like that, Zahra? How do you feel like when you come to Canada?" I told them, "To be honest I would rather be in [a] Muslim nation, and I would rather be in [a] Muslim country, but [it is] only [because of] circumstances that I am doing this. If I have the opportunity, I would stay with my own people, my own country [sighs].

Zahra claims she was harassed because of her religion and also sexually harassed by white workers at the shelter.

Zahra: In the smoking room I used to go and have a cigarette, and they came and sometimes touch my neck, kiss me, and I was really very uncomfortable. They harass[ed] me, and they say [sic] that they know I am a lesbian. . . . And they ask [sic] me questions and personal stuff which has nothing to do with business. . . . It was white women.[15]

Zahra took her complaints to the board of the shelter, but she says that she was outnumbered. As bell hooks (1993) argues, black women often have to suffer in silence in environments that are dominated by white people, as it is not safe for them to express their objections, concerns, and outrage. Zahra did not feel safe because she was one of the few women of color in a room full of white women. It is significant that Zahra grew up in Somalia, a country torn by civil war, yet in Canada her notions of not feeling safe centered around her being categorized as black and Muslim. The shelter management told her to leave the shelter:

> Zahra: They told me, "You can't stay and wait for your vehicle." . . . I said, "You guys, I haven't been fired, and I am still working here, so what is this?" . . . They said, "Hey, Zahra, you better listen." So I left the office. I was in a bad mood. I go [sic], and I attempted suicide.

Although Zahra is translating and negotiating from a third space, the lack of support in expressing herself in Canada culminated at one moment in her life in a suicide attempt. She finds no space from which to express herself as a Somali and as a Muslim woman. Instead she finds that all she stands for and believes in is devalued.

> Zahra: It is not something you have to do. It is something that is inside. What you believe. . . . But where are you going to express yourself? Where are you going to do these things? . . . This is what really makes me sick at the society and at the system. How are we going to work out all those things? How are we going to survive? I find, there is [sic] a lot of Muslim women. There is a lot of [different] cultural [sic] people who need somebody who understands to work with them. How can we help them, all those people? They allow them to come to Canada, but did they provide somebody to work with them? No, they are just brought and dumped here. They can't really figure out white middle-class women or men working at immigration. When you go there, first they should tell you, "Oh, we are not accepting any more refugees" or "We don't need any African people." It makes me feel really sad. If I have a chance, believe me, I will go back to my country—if it is safe, and there is no war. . . . In this country I am just losing energy, self-esteem. It makes you scared sometimes.

The way in which the categorization of Muslim woman is played out at the shelter and in the Somali community puts her in a bind, pushed and pulled in different directions. She objects to, and at the same defends and wants to embrace Muslim female identity. Her emotional dissonance finds no place of legitimization and leads to despair and fear for her future.

Kausar

Kausar's history is one of migration and diasporic dislocation, where home evokes a place of roots and a place of sojournment. Her negotiations in this continuous history of displacement indicate that she is in the third space. Kausar is brown-skinned and originally from India. Her family migrated to East Pakistan during the partition of India and Pakistan in 1947. Yet another partition, this time of Pakistan and Bangladesh in 1971, made them move to Karachi, in what is now left of Pakistan. Kausar moved again, this time to the Gulf States with her husband, and finally to Canada in 1991.

Kausar comes from a political and religious family who fought the British assault on Indian Muslim culture in pre-partition India.

Kausar: My grandfather had aligned himself with Gandhi, and also in our house in India, there is this room where Gandhi used to come and stay. And [there is] this *khoonta* you know, the nail where he used to tie his goat. And so they were very much anti-British and anti-West and very very nationalistic. And of course then they opted to fight for Pakistan, and so my father, he wasn't even allowed to go to a Western type of [educational] institution.

Because her father did not want to be left out of political events, he secretly taught himself English by reading newspapers. Kausar says her father also realized that the Indian cultural/political "order was crumbling." The only way for his family to be equipped for the challenges that lay ahead in the subcontinent and have any input in their resolution was for his children to acquire westernized education.

Thus Kausar and her sister, although they came from an anti-West family, attended an English-medium private school for girls in Bangladesh. At school Kausar was taught that the British conquest of India was benign and that it "brought about a lot of reforms and people's lives were made better because of it." European culture was emphasized as superior and liberal compared to Pakistani culture. Polygamy and purdah were particularly held up as indicative of the "barbaric" nature of Islamic practices.[16] In contrast, gender relations were deemed to be fair and equal in Western culture. Kausar later went on to the same school in Karachi that Zubaida and I also attended. The messages we received there emphasized Christianity as a civilizing force with the nuns as its agents.[17]

In Kausar's home Indian/Pakistani Muslim culture was prized, while at school it was devalued by the Western norms that were being emphasized. These contradictory messages created considerable dissonance between home and school, and she recalls that "there were two worlds when I was growing up." For instance, her older sister had to wear a *burkha* to their anglicized school and suffered teasing and scorn from other anglicized Pakistani girls for her more traditional dress.[18] When her sister told their parents that she did not want to wear a *burkha* at school, she was given a choice to either wear it and stay at that school or to go to another school where wearing a *burkha* was more accepted. She chose to stay at the westernized school and wear the *burkha*. It is significant that even at the age of nine, the child appears to have realized that the westernized school was somehow more advantageous to her than the indigenous one, even when tainted with harassment by her peers. Kausar successfully fought against having to wear the *burkha* but had to agree to wear a *shalwar* with the uniform, which was a skirt. The other girls at the school made fun of Kausar and her sister and marginalized them for being different and "not modern." Although she did not realize it then, Kausar now believes there was implicit pressure from peers and teachers on her and her sister to prove themselves and legitimize their difference. This added pressure may be one of the reasons they did so well at school. An unfortunate aspect of this westernization, Kausar claims, is that her Urdu is not as good as her English.

Kausar realizes that partly because of her education, she has equated westernization with being more liberal, more competent, more efficient, and better able to succeed in contemporary societies. Her ten years in the Gulf States substantiated this type of reasoning and proved to her that westernization was quite advantageous. In the Gulf States, she claims, being Muslim did not matter. Being westernized, however, was advantageous, particularly when seeking employment.

She believes she may have decided to come to Canada because it was a natural progression of the "West is best" philosophy. Once in Canada, however, Kausar realized that although her knowledge of Western culture had opened limited doors for her in employment, it had not prevented her from being excluded and marginalized in the dominant society.

Kausar: I feel that maybe . . . we have been deluded all along, [by] westernization and the media and everything, that this is a better place to be. It is an ideal if you can go to the West.

At this point in her life, the nature of her work causes her to rethink some of the messages she received through her education and in the milieu in which she lived in Pakistan:

Kausar: Where I am working . . . on anti-racism . . . the place to start is to see where we are and why we are where we are, and that made me think a lot about my background and my history and upbringing. I can see that a lot of my earlier life was a reaction, or wanting to be as western-ized as possible.

In Canada, Kausar asserts that she is positioned as a South Asian. Yet her family history of anticolonial struggles, as well as her location in anti-Muslim society, influences her decision to position herself as a Muslim woman as well. She identifies as a Muslim in Canada more than she did in the Muslim countries she had lived in before, namely Pakistan and a few of the Gulf States:

Kausar: The multicultural state puts you into categories, a sort of trap. People identify me as a South Asian because of my skin color and my features, but I feel that I have to identify myself as a South Asian Muslim woman all the time in Canada. I am reacting as a Muslim. I feel there is a need for this which was not there in Pakistan or the Gulf. I am not religious, but being Muslim is considered derogatory, and I am not ashamed to be a Muslim. And I say, "Why should I not identify myself as a Muslim?"

Shahnaz: Did you feel it [being a Muslim] is under attack here?

Kausar: Yes, and I have to assert it.

Floya Anthias and Nira Yuval-Davis (1983) argue that diverse and some-times contradictory ideological discourses divide people into collectives. The boundaries of these collectives overlap or shift. Since conventional wisdom deems that all Muslims are Arabs, Kausar (who is from Pakistan) is considered South Asian before she is considered Muslim. She identifies as a South Asian Muslim partly in reaction to anti-Muslim sentiments in Canada that are not necessarily directed at her.

However, in identifying herself as a member of the Muslim collective, Kausar faces a dilemma. Defending Islam involves defending negative elements she says she fears. Yuval-Davis (1994) points to this as a di-lemma faced by many women: "Often, the particular culture they would like to assert vis-à-vis the hegemonic culture also includes elements which they feel subordinate them as women and which they would like to resist and transform within their own communities" (414).

For instance, although Kausar identifies herself as a Muslim, it is not an unqualified identification.

Kausar: I don't go near organized Islamic communities.

Shahnaz: Why?

Kausar: It scares me.

Shahnaz: What scares you?

Kausar: I have found them very self-righteous.

Also she is reevaluating her position about Islam. She knows that there is more to be being Muslim than prescriptions, but she feels constrained in expressing her criticisms. When asked about the proposal to have *Shari'a* in Canada, she replies:

Kausar: I opposed it strongly. . . . I don't think we need it.

Shahnaz: But there are those that equate *Shari'a* law with God's law.

Kausar: I don't agree with that. Because . . . I am not sure what is a good Muslim.

Shahnaz: So you think *Shari'a* is a construct.

Kausar: Yeah, it could be.

Shahnaz: It could be?

Kausar: I don't want to say it on tape. I don't know what the consequences might be.

She reminded me of the current situation in Pakistan where speaking out against Islam or even being suspected of doing so has severe ramifications.[19] Kausar stated that her family is in Pakistan, and she also goes to visit there, so she is cautious about what she says.

Positioning herself as a Muslim woman for Kausar means that she has to mother Muslim children. This places tremendous pressure on her. Her family is in Pakistan, and she is not connected to the Islamic community in Canada. Thus Kausar has to assume the responsibility of instilling a cultural identity in her children within the nuclear family.

Kausar: I feel that I have become closer to them in a sense because I feel more protective. I feel very responsible for bringing them here. I looked into organized Islamic classes, and I did force my son to go. I have read the *Qur'an* in Arabic, and I feel that he should read it.

Shahnaz: You feel it is more important here than it is in Pakistan?

Kausar: Otherwise I don't know where he will place himself. He will be like a person without an identity. I gave up on the *Qur'an* idea because my son is against it. I don't think it is the *Qur'an* that he is against, but he just felt that the atmosphere was such . . . he didn't want to go anymore.

Kausar is concerned about her son's sense of location, but she is also reevaluating her assumptions, for instance her lifelong equation of westernization and modernity with progressive, competence, and efficiency.

She also realizes that her father embodies some of the contradictions that result when modernity and tradition are set up as binary opposites:

Kausar: He was considered very, very conservative by all our friends, and we all thought that he was extremely conservative. But now that I look back I realize that in certain ways he was much more liberal than many of my friends' fathers were. . . . In education, he never stopped us from whatever we felt like studying. A lot of his friends tried to discourage him who were very westernized, and who had married westernized Muslim women.

Shahnaz: [Talking about your father], it seems that you are equating Westernism with liberalism.

Kausar: I realize that I did that all my life. I mean for a great part of my life.

Shahnaz: And you got that from school?

Kausar: And I got that from the society which was developing around me. It was not just school—my friends and my father's friends. . . . Definitely it was the school. . . . If you are westernized, you are considered more liberal.

Kausar realizes that the binary opposition of such concepts as modern/liberal and traditional/conservative needs to be rethought, especially the message that "If you are westernized, you are considered more competent."

Similar to Iram, Kausar opposes the self-righteousness of Islamic organizations but defends herself as a Muslim in reaction to racism. Yet there are also differences. Iram grew up in Canada, and the racism she faced made her doubt the "West is best" message. Kausar learned "West is best" through her education, and this idea was reinforced in the Gulf States. Her experiences in Canada finally disrupted this message. In particular, Kausar's search for employment in Canada triggered a reflexive response to her westernized education. She realized that her assumptions about equality and fairness in the West needed to be reevaluated. Although Kausar, in her capacity as a journalist, has covered international events in the Middle East, her capability and experience were not valued in Canada.

Kausar: I worked for an international news agency [in the Gulf], and when I left, they told me that I had done a good job, and they were very happy with the way I worked. I had covered press conferences and all kinds of world leaders. But here I was really made to feel as if I knew nothing, and my experience did not count for anything. I don't know. I almost started believing it. . . . A few did call me for interviews. When I went there, I realized that the only thing they felt that I . . . had any authority to write about was if there was any issue about Pakistan. And about women, or Islam, or rape, or such.

Kausar's broader experience did not appear to have any value, and she was ghettoized. It seems to be the prevalent belief in Canadian society that women of color can know only about issues of other women of color, not about all women.[20] Neither are they judged competent to write about global issues that are not gender focused.

Kausar pointed out that her employment search experience has really shaken her confidence. She has begun to question the requirement of Canadian experience and thinks it is a major obstacle to her getting a job.

Shahnaz: Do you think it is a big issue?

Kausar: Well, it is at least presented as a big issue.

Shahnaz: Do you think that it is necessary?

Kausar: I don't think so.

Yet Kausar says at times she "almost started believing" that she does not have the required competence. When I brought up the possibility of shifting some personal blame to structures in society that work to marginalize certain groups, Kausar voiced a concern similar to Rabia's.

Kausar: I have been thinking . . . that a lot of it is also my own upbringing. Because . . . you are always made to look at yourself through other people's eyes.

Shahnaz: So you are saying that our upbringing is not necessarily productive for us here?

Kausar: Absolutely. It is not productive. . . . All the struggles that I have had in coming here, and yet you could say that it was a passive kind of life because I was always looking at . . . what I should be instead of what I am. And always looking at *laug kaya kahange* [what will people say].

Kausar, like Rabia, agreed that such reasoning was extremely detrimental to living in Canada, particularly since they have had a liberal education, which encourages them to keep looking for flaws within themselves and not at the system.

Kausar is also suspicious of the forums provided by the multicultural state for women from different communities, particularly those that critique sexism. Because of stereotypes about the oppression of Muslim women, what individual women say, Kausar argues, can be used to reinforce biases about Islam and Muslims.

Shahnaz: How does it impact on you when you see stereotypes of Muslim women?

Kausar: It bothers me.

Shahnaz: What are some of the stereotypes that bother you?

Kausar: One of them is women accepting passively that men are free to marry four wives. It is quite strange. I guess because of the insensitivity to some of these things, I identify myself as a Muslim woman. I feel that I have every right to say my prayers as I want and not follow these organized groups.

As Kausar reacts to Orientalist/racist stereotypes and identifies herself as a Muslim woman, she is confronted by the way the Muslim woman is structured within Islamist discourse. She refuses to accept their vision for her. Instead she challenges them and argues that she will decide how and what she will follow in Islam. In so doing she attempts to restructure herself in a third space where she is making different assumptions and rereading received knowledge. She asserts that she is at a stage in her life where she is rethinking many things.

Kausar: I feel that maybe because we have been deluded all along by the westernization and the media and everything that this is a better place to be. It is an ideal if you can go to the West. I am still trying to think about it. I have felt very shaken and hurt, demoralized and depressed, everything.

Kausar recognizes and names the contradictions in her life. Her attempts to resolve these contradictions give rise to expressions of emotional ambivalence and disorientation. Her own location within multiculturalism in Canada seems to be a trap with no way out, producing disillusionment, demoralization, and despair. Although she is negotiating her life as a hybridized individual, her account suggests a desire for stability. Her history of continued migration and dislocation no doubt contributes to this disorientation. And she is on the move again. Her husband could not find work in Canada, and recently the family moved back to the Gulf States.

Nabia

Nabia was born in Egypt in 1958 to an upper-class family and was thirty-four at the time of the interview. She lived in Egypt until 1979 and then moved to Canada with her brother to join her mother who had moved here and married an Anglo-Canadian. Previously they had lived with their grandparents in Cairo. Nabia went to a private school, a lycée, in Cairo. Before the revolution that brought Nasser to power in 1952, such schools were totally French, but now the curriculum is divided between French and Arabic. French teachers came from France and taught at the school. Nabia says that she was quite a "Francophile" because she read a lot of French and knew a lot about French culture and literature. It was considered the chic thing to do in the circles in which she moved. Nabia claims the Arabic teachers at her school were not as good as the French teachers; the Arabic teachers emphasized rote learning. The curriculum was not structured in a way to make the Arabic literature as appealing as the French.

Upon graduating from school she went to Cairo University and earned her B.A. in Islamic archaeology. Nabia claims her choosing Islamic rather than Egyptian archaeology was an aesthetic choice. She wanted to work with monuments that were standing and not have to sift through sand dunes. While at the private school, she had met people from her own social class, but at the university she came across people from a broader spectrum of life.

Nabia's grandmother was determined to get her married, and thus Nabia was quite glad to move to Canada in 1979:

> Nabia: My grandmother was trying to marry me off unsuccessfully. The last year I was there she was really keen on getting me married, and I told my grandfather that I was really interested in my education and I wasn't ready to get married. He stood by me, and he said, "stop" to her. . . . And my mother wrote to her and said "my girl ain't going to get married just because you want her to get married." Once in a while she would say, "When are you getting married?" It was a big issue, and now I am an old maid [laughs], and she is really upset. But she doesn't show it as much as she used to.

In Canada she earned an M.A. and then a Ph.D. in Islamic studies. She has just completed a postdoctorate degree in Islamic studies and works in a large cultural/educational institution in the United States.

As a scholar of Islamic studies, Nabia is quite familiar with the historically structured discourses and the contradictions that are embedded in the category Muslim woman.

> Shahnaz: When did you become aware of becoming "the Muslim woman"?
>
> Nabia: "The Muslim woman." At the university in Canada, although it took a while. The first two years I was trying to find my way around. I

didn't think it through. When somebody would make a comment, I would think of the answer two days later.

Shahnaz: What kind of comment?

Nabia: Of being different or coming from "over there." . . . You know the quizzical look, and people won't say much, actually, and people will say, "Oh, you are from Egypt, oh," and there is a big silence. That will be the end of the conversation. One time I was in class, and a girl who had gone to Israel was making comments about how . . . she had gone to a game and people were cheering, and all the swear words were in Arabic, because Hebrew didn't have swear words. And then there was this big silence to see what was my response.

Shahnaz: So you were supposed to represent the whole Arab world?

Nabia: Exactly.

Shahnaz: What was your response?

Nabia: Oh, I said that Arabic was a richer language [laughs] and contains many imaginative swear words, and that was the end of the conversation of course. You get comments like, "But you don't look Egyptian." Well, how do you know if I look Egyptian? . . . They assume that Muslim women are all covered up. I mean again this stereotype [of] a certain coloring. I am not that fair, but for them my eyes are hazel, so they assume [I] must be sort of Christian being fair. It is funny, but in Egypt Christians are much darker than Muslims.

Although Nabia states she has developed a quick response to stereotypical comments, there are situations where race and gender combine to produce interesting dynamics. Sometimes her colleagues are experts in historical Islamic studies but have little knowledge of current events. On an archaeological dig in an Arab country, she was placed in the position of cultural interpreter.

Nabia: I went with one of my professors who had worked in Iran but . . . didn't know any Arabic, and so had to depend on me to communicate. His male chauvinism came out. . . . He couldn't stand a woman speaking for him. I was happy because he was threatened by an Arab Muslim woman. With what you were saying earlier about Islamic experts having knowledge abut medieval archaeology but not about day-to-day life, actually I had to extricate him from certain situations where he made an ass of himself.

Shahnaz: It must have been difficult.

Nabia: Yes. . . . It was challenging. . . . I have lots of stories. Later when we were colleagues, . . . he accused me of playing the Middle Eastern woman.

Shahnaz: Middle Eastern woman?

Nabia: I can't remember the exact words that he used, but that I was playing the Middle Eastern woman, who was not assertive. And I said, "How dare [he] say this?" having worked with him all these years. You Western men, [I thought], I would rather deal with Middle Eastern men because their male chauvinism I can deal with. It comes out straight away. But you do it in a sneaky way.

Shahnaz: What do you think he meant by the term Middle Eastern woman?

Nabia: He meant I was trying to get my way . . . [by] manipulating.

Nabia is angered, because of how little the "expert" on Islam knows about everyday life in Muslim countries and because in his interactions with her he is not responding to her but to stereotypes about the Middle Eastern / Muslim woman.

Nabia also feels stereotyped in her personal relationships with men.

Nabia: They [men] think, "How can I relate to her?" Especially if it is a non-Arab man.

Shahnaz: Do you find that they [men] are on their guard?

Nabia: Yes, they are . . . because they don't know in matters of, I guess, sexuality.

Shahnaz: Of how they should be approaching you.

Nabia: Yes, yes.

Shahnaz: Do you think they are responding to you or do you think they are responding to the TV Muslim woman?

Nabia: Initially the TV . . . which is the veil, but I don't wear one.

Shahnaz: Do you think at any point they respond to Nabia?

Nabia: Oh, yes, I hope they respond to me as a person.

Shahnaz: Do you think there is some sort of interconnecting [they are doing] between the stereotype and you?

Nabia: Not always, but often . . . whether [because I am Muslim] I would be willing to go to bed with them or not.

Although Nabia is positioned as a Muslim woman within dominant culture, she disavows Muslim identity based on active religious community participation. Instead Nabia embraces an intellectual, objective interest in studying Islam as a culture. Speaking of how Muslims position themselves in North America, she says:

Nabia: The way I see it is that it [rules] is the way they [Muslims in Canada] define their own identity, in terms of religious cultural heritage.

Shahnaz: With prescriptions?

Nabia: Yes.

Shahnaz: Do you think that it has to do with the pressures of being a minority?

Nabia: I think so.

Shahnaz: And how are you defining your identity?

Nabia: [silence]

Shahnaz: You are obviously not defining it by saying your prayers.

Nabia: I guess I am defining it by studying my own culture. I have chosen to do that in a way. I made a choice back home when I was still in Egypt, when people assumed that I would choose to study French literature or do something that is more marketable in their minds. I mean going to Islamic archaeology was not looked upon as being very prestigious, and in that sense I was choosing what I wanted to do and making my own statement. Coming here and continuing in that field and being in a different society—again maybe my choice was being different. I was different there and different here.

Although Nabia has knowledge of all the determinations of the Muslim woman, she is emphasizing only one aspect of difference, Islamist prescriptions. Yet in her everyday interactions and in her personal life, she is responded to as a Muslim woman. So while she does not want to be a part of Muslim identity as it exists in North America, she cannot disavow being a Muslim unless she disavows her entire personal and professional history. Thus, Nabia confronts the contradictions of the category Muslim woman and disavows any containment within a Muslim identity.

In Nabia's case, anti-Muslim stereotypes as well Islamist visions for the Muslim woman led her to invest in an identity that for her is basically negative. However, because she is a cultural worker involved in the ongoing production of Islamic identity, I had certain expectations of her. Before the interview began, I pointed out that I would be asking her about her sense of herself as a Muslim woman in Canada. She had replied, "As a Muslim woman, uhum, I have hit a blank."

Shahnaz: Earlier you said to me, "I hit a blank," and [reminded me] that you were focusing on the restrictive practices, and I pointed to your own active interest in the area. I want you to expand on this.

Nabia: Back to the blank.

Shahnaz: Why was it that you hit a blank?

Nabia: I think it is because every time, not every time, but often, being a Muslim means rules and regulations.

Shahnaz: However, a person in your field with the amount of knowledge that you possess, which is far more than anything that I know because you continuously read on this topic while I work in women's studies, . . . the restrictive practices are a very small part of it.

Nabia: Small part of it, yes. But what else is there?

Shahnaz: You tell me.

Nabia: I don't know [emphasis].

Shahnaz: If you don't know, who would know?

Nabia: I just live my life!

Shahnaz: The civilization, the class issue, the art, the music, the poetry, the literature, the architecture, the sense of self that comes from all of this.

Nabia: Right. . . . Right, but we are living in a country where there is none of this.

Shahnaz: That is why somebody of your background is very important. I need to be able to come to you, and you need to be able to give this sense to me.

Nabia: Right, right, I am having a hard time. I don't know why I am having a hard time getting this out.

Shahnaz: I guess I am feeling frustrated that I have to extract it.

Nabia: I may have just blocked it out. I mean obviously I have blocked it out. These are issues that I haven't thought about. You are making me think about them.

From this sequence it becomes evident that the interaction between Nabia and myself was a co-construction. I was making discursive demands on Nabia to which she was unable to respond. I wanted her to identify a particular cultural formation within which she affirms herself as a Muslim woman without subscribing to Islamism. Although Nabia was producing knowledge that would be part of such a movement, she would not or could not point me to such a cultural formation. I was looking to Nabia to help me resolve my own ambivalence, while she was in a situation where she could not resolve her own. I ended up feeling frustrated because she was as ambivalent as I was.

For Nabia, the vision of an essentialized Muslim woman prevails. In her resistance of the stereotypical assumptions as well as prescriptions for authenticity, she rejects and disavows the claim of the image on her. She claims that she blanked out because "I thought of prayers and fasting, which I don't do." Nabia is not devout according to Islamist requirements and, therefore, does not consider herself Muslim. As a cultural worker and a presumed spokesperson for the Muslim woman, Nabia is in an ambivalent position. She responds to that ambivalence by "blanking out" and disengaging from her understanding of Muslim identity in Canada, engaging instead with the past.

> Shahnaz: I find that scholars of Islamic studies are often quite well-briefed in medieval issues and ancient stuff, but they are not keen to take on modern issues. They find that too controversial. Do you find that in the people that you are working with?
>
> Nabia: Yes, yes.
>
> Shahnaz: Why do you think that is so?
>
> Nabia: Well, . . . it is . . . much safer than to deal with the newer stuff.
>
> Shahnaz: If they deal with the current stuff, they have to confront racism.
>
> Nabia: Yes.
>
> Shahnaz: Do you think that it is an issue for you as well?
>
> Nabia: Maybe, it could be. I hadn't thought about it, but it is possible.

Nabia finds archaeology less controversial than dealing with the current politics of the Muslim woman. Conventional articulations of Islamic identity are increasingly defined in essentialist terms in the polarities of Islamism and Orientalism. Perhpas Nabia "blanks out" because she cannot self-identify within the negativity of Orientalism and yet is not able to find a way of expressing her Muslim identity in North America, which is distinct from versions of Islamism. She is nevertheless in the position of being a spokesperson for the "Muslim woman" and is implicated in the ongoing production of contemporary Islamic identity, but she does not see herself in this way. She sees herself as an archaeologist. When I expressed my frustration and challenged her "inability" to provide me with cultural affirmation, Nabia became noticeably unsettled. At the end of the interview she promised to call me back after she had thought about the implications of our conversation. We talked two days later.

> Nabia: I have chosen my field not out of a sense of mission, but because it was my area of interest. I do not think I have done it out of a reaction to my life in Canada.

Nabia's response suggests that her choice is unconnected to the social and political system in which she works and lives. She seems to have gone back to her original position and reiterated that she was doing archaeology because of personal interest. She is producing knowledge and materials that could be a part of a broader cultural affirmation for Muslims. Despite my expectations and challenges, she refuses to position herself as a leader or even an active participant in an Islamic cultural movement. Her account strikes me as an interesting attempt to be apolitical, as one who is knowledgeable but dispassionate, a neutral conduit of knowledge about Islam. Nabia leaves me wondering if this is the price of "success" for a Muslim woman academic in the field of Islamic archaeology.

Selecting What to Believe

The often contradictory determinations influencing how Muslim female identity is categorized and coded entice as well as distance individual women from being Muslim in Canada. In enacting their Muslim identity, women not only confront the sexist regulations within their own communities but also the racist and sexist stereotyping and marginalization of Muslim women in the larger community. Thus being Muslim in Canada is not only a spiritual experience but is also, in part, a reactive stance, a product of a colonial-racist situation. The women's stories indicate that to practice Muslim identity seems to have more significance in Canada (a non-Muslim, even anti-Muslim society) than in the women's countries of origin. Many of the women I interviewed are reading the *Qur'an* in Canada with interpretations and analyses, which they had not done in their countries of origin.[1]

The narratives elaborated in this chapter suggest that the women have accepted the linking of their identity as Muslim women with a discourse heavily influenced by prescriptions. Yet while they accept such determinations of their identity, they are also able to critique their internal contradictions. To resolve the contradictions generated by their desire for equality with men and their need to address the sexism they encounter in Islam, they focus on what they believe is the intent of the Islamic message and not on the sexist practices. Manal, Tuzeen, and Donna's stories suggest that they are very clear about their Muslim identity. If they express emotional dissonance, it is about particular communal practices in which their identity is rooted.

Manal

Manal is fair-skinned and was born in Egypt in 1959. She came to Canada in 1974 when she was twenty-five years old. Manal went to a public school in Egypt where the medium of instruction was Arabic, and English was taught as a foreign language from grade seven onward. In her school, Manal recalls, "education was based on Arabic culture and the Islamic culture," in which the role of the woman as nurturer of the family was stressed.

This focus on the woman as nurturer was also stressed at home. Manal points out that although her parents were very trusting, there were also a lot of rules, such as "no sleeping over" at other people's places and "no evening parties." Because the values stressed at school and at home were basically the same, Manal found little dissonance between the messages received at school, home, and the society that she lived in. While the focus in the school she attended was Islamic and Arab culture, European art and design were stressed at university.

Manal met her husband at university. He wanted her to start a dating relationship with him, but she said:

> Manal: I am not the kind of girl that will go out with you. No dating or anything. . . . And then he came to my parents' house, and he talked to my father, and we got engaged in second-year university and married in the fourth year.

She received her B.A. in Egypt and began to work in a museum as a guide. Her husband had family in Canada, and they encouraged the couple to immigrate here. Initially she was excited about coming to Canada and thought that they would live here for about five years and then go back to Egypt. Twenty-two years later they are still here.

Manal positions herself as a Muslim in Canada much more than she ever did in Egypt.

> Shahnaz: What did it mean for you to be Muslim in Egypt?
>
> Manal: It was natural.
>
> Shahnaz: You never thought about it?
>
> Manal: Because everything around you was the same. You are in your home, you hear the call for prayer five times a day, and you get up and do it. In Ramadan everybody is fasting, and nobody has the courage to go out and eat.

In Canada it is not the same. Trinh Minh-Ha (1989) notes that construction of difference goes hand in hand with a sense of the fragility of difference, which has to be defended and maintained. As a Muslim woman Manal is constructed as different in Canada. The difference, however, is fragmented and fragile. "You have to work a little bit harder here to keep your habits," she says.

As Manal locates herself as a Muslim in Canada, she accepts prescriptions for the Muslim woman, noting few contradictions. The *hejab* has a central position in these prescriptions. Manal never wore one in Egypt. She was part of the milieu, and her identity was not threatened. Manal says she feels the need to wear the *hejab* in Canada, however. In wearing the *hejab*, Manal visibly identifies herself as Muslim. As she enacts her Muslim identity, she confronts stereotypes, particularly in the media, about Muslims and the Muslim woman.

> Manal: In TV [there are] lots of programs . . . they show that Arabs and Muslims are really undeveloped people. I don't want to go into politics, but I see how they [media] treat the Arabs and Muslims and how they treat the non-Arabs and non-Muslims, and it makes me very angry.

Manal objects to the media's depictions of Muslims and is especially concerned about reports focusing on Palestine and Israel. Yet in her disassociation—"I am not a fanatic Muslim"—she validates the stereotypes as well. For her the stereotypes represent two poles: desire to be recognized and aversion to the person so recognized.

> Manal: We are hearing in the media now "fanatics, fundamentalists, and terrorists."
>
> Shahnaz: What do "fanatic" and "fundamentalist" mean to you?
>
> Manal: I know that means you go by the rules strictly and nothing else. You don't even think.

She admits that she got this impression of fanatic and fundamentalist Muslims from the media in Canada. She knows very few Muslims like that either in Egypt or here in Canada. Bruce Lawrence (1987) has argued that fundamentalism is not a term Muslims use either for their own religion or that of others. Yet Manal does use the term to describe those who are different from her. And fundamentalists are those who are presented to her through Canadian media. She claims they are unlike anyone she knows personally but admits they exist, insisting that she is not one of them and wants no part of them. Her response suggests an aversion to and disavowal of the stereotypical Muslim.

Although to an extent Manal appears to accept the popular vision of Muslims, she was definitely not in agreement with popular images of the Muslim woman. She stated emphatically that the media were not fair and that women had more rights in Islamic societies than in secular Canada.

> Shahnaz: What does it do for you when you see on TV that Muslims are fanatic and fundamentalist and that [Muslim] women are oppressed.
>
> Manal: That is not fair.

Shahnaz: Do you feel oppressed?

Manal: No I am not. I feel that Muslim women have more rights than . . . Canadian [women].

Shahnaz: In which ways do Muslim women have more rights?

Manal: First, we have the right to carry our own name. The first thing that I did here was to change my name.[2]

Shahnaz: Why did you change it?

Manal: Because it was too much trouble. All the mail or the taxes and everything had to be connected to the husband, "Mr. and Mrs.," last name and first name.

Shahnaz: What else?

Manal: Also the voting. We had the vote even before Canada and the [United] States. . . . Also, if you own something before you get married, if you own a house, it is yours.[3] . . . And you can have divorce if you want.

Manal believes in the importance of Islam to ensure the rights of Muslim women. She is clear about her Muslim identity and believes that it is workable in Canada. Yet, as Frigga Haug points out that "the absence of contradiction in our self-interpretations will to a large extent be constructed by us; contradictions are forgotten and omitted, left unperceived, while to a degree, it is our use of such constructions that enables us to get by in the world, they ultimately prevent us from gaining a proper grip on reality" (Haug 1987, 40). Manal's sense of the contradictions and the ambivalence in her life is minimal. She truly believes that Islamic rules and prescriptions can provide resolutions to everyday situations.

Manal believes that if people followed Islam, there would be no violence in the home. Her references to abuse in a relative's family provide an example.

Manal: I disagree with violence, but it is happening, and it happened with one of my husband's relatives. She was here with no sister, no father, or no family except us. Her husband used to hit her in front of her kids. I took her to a shelter. We tried to talk to her. Every day we talked until four or five in the morning; my husband and I talked to both of them. She called the police, and they took her to a shelter, and then she went back to him.

Shahnaz: What happened to her?

Manal: I don't know. I am not in touch with her. I am fed up.

Shahnaz: It is not easy to leave your husband. . . . She may not be used to living alone.

Manal: But she was not alone. She has three kids. The system here, they provide her with a house and with welfare money. She says that the kids need the father. She sacrificed herself for the kids.

Shahnaz: What would you like to see happen when there is violence in a home?

Manal: I would like it to stop, and [the] family [to] stay together. If everyone brings up the family in the right way, the way Islam says, then there will be no violence.

Shahnaz: So you think that people are not following the proper Islamic values [and] that is why there is violence?

Manal: Yes.

Unlike Zahra, Manal has had only positive experience with Canadian agencies. Manal believes that a women's shelter can take the place of the support of family for an abused woman. Muslim women, she believes, do not need to stay in an abusive situation in Canada because of the social support network. She is upset that her relative went back to the husband. Moreover, Manal believes that if people followed Islam, there would be no violence in the home. Deemphasizing a sura in the *Qur'an* that says men can beat disobedient wives, Manal sets up an ideal situation in which both women and men follow the *Qur'an*, resulting in no violence.[4] Such a utopian ideal helps strengthen the fragility of her Muslim difference in Canada. It also allows her to confront in a practical way the sexism and male violence within her community. So while she blames the man for his violent behavior, she would also implicitly blame the woman if she were unfaithful. Speaking of divorce, Manal claims that "if the woman is faithful, obeys him [husband], cares for family or kids, it is his fault." When people are not practicing the "ideal," she gives up on the situation.

Manal's sense of Muslim female identity also includes Muslim mothering. She claims that "I have to watch my kids and their friends." In particular she is trying to extend her vision of the Muslim woman to her daughters:

Manal: I tell them that they are not allowed to have boyfriends. . . . They can have friends, boys and girls, as long as they are in a group . . . [not] alone together.

Shahnaz: What about boys?

> Manal: I will tell my son when he grows up to keep the girls exactly the same way that other boys keep his sisters.

Connecting the Muslim woman's morality with her community's morality, Manal is focusing on the virtue of women. The message for her son is that he is to watch out for his sister and the sisters of other men.

Manal's story indicates that she believes in the prescriptions for Muslim woman as well as a need to enact them in Canada. She is prepared to name and challenge the process of her othering. The only aspect of the contradictions with the categorization Muslim woman that she names is the uncertainty or doubt she expresses around *Shari'a*. She stated that although some men would abuse it:

> Manal: I think it would be good for Muslims in general.
>
> Shahnaz: Why?
>
> Manal: I can't tell you why, but we go by the *Qur'an*.

The centrality of *Shari'a* in the Islamist construction of identity for the Muslim woman has been well documented.[5] I have previously argued that the desire for such an identity pits women against the "Islamic" community in Canada (Khan 1993). Although Manal appears to accept the centrality of *Shari'a* as integral to her being Muslim, her response suggests unresolved emotional dissonance. Despite the acknowledgement that it can be used by men to abuse women, she claims that it is the "will of God" and "we [Muslims] go by the *Qur'an*." When I asked her to elaborate, she could not do so. Manal appears to accept the value of *Shari'a* as leap of faith, thus leaving no room for contradictions. She referred me to an Egyptian scholar who she claimed had a lot of knowledge about Islam and perhaps could explain the value of *Shari'a* to me.

All the other fifteen women acknowledge contradictions in their lives between self-identifying and being responded to as Muslim. Manal is different. She is the one most invested in enacting what appears to be a non-contradictory Muslim identity. Within her narrative of migration and loss of family networks, perhaps this ideal identity provides for her a fixity in the hybridized postcolonial space of displacement in which she is positioned. She admits to no contradictions. Even those contradictions she does acknowledge, around *Shari'a*, she defers to an Islamic authority.

Tuzeen

Tuzeen is white-skinned and was born in India in 1946. She moved to Pakistan in 1950, and at the age of eighteen, in 1964, she married a cousin and went to live in Sydney, Australia, where her husband was finishing his education. In 1970 she and her husband and two children immigrated to Canada.

Tuzeen went to schools where the language of instruction was Urdu and English was taught as a specific subject. In history class they focused on the history of India during the Mughal rule. Tuzeen's school also had religious education. They learned prayer and the rights and roles of Muslims. Although Tuzeen's school did have a uniform, of which the *dupatta* formed a part, she does not recall ever having been forced to cover her head either at school or at home. She remembers such restrictions came later: "after Bhutto came . . . those things came up." Tuzeen states that if she had been forced to cover her head, she would have considered it a restriction. She also does not remember being forced to observe religious prescriptions. "My father, it didn't matter to him. My mother would teach us everything, especially covering the head. She never force [*sic*] us. She just tell [*sic*] us that 'You know my job is to tell you, and it is up to you whether you do it or not'." Tuzeen remembers little difference between the worlds that she lived in at home and at school in terms of the cultural messages she received.

Like Manal, Tuzeen is very clear about her identity as a Muslim woman in Canada. Islam provides her with spiritual stability as well as continuity with her Muslim upbringing in a society where, despite having white skin, her difference is not welcome. Tuzeen encounters stereotypical assumptions about Muslims and about Muslim women in particular:

Shahnaz: What do you think of images we see on TV about Muslim women, how we are all oppressed by religion and how we have to cover our heads?

Tuzeen: That is where I have discussions with my Canadian friends. They ask me questions about the four marriages.[6] [It is the] first question. And I said, "Yes, it is a law but not the way you people think it is." Then I explain that it is a law under very special circumstances. They ask me a lot about Khomeini. When I was working, it was hot news, and everybody say [*sic*], "Did you read the paper today? Did you see this?" People say this because they don't know Islam.

As Tuzeen explains Islam to her friends, she also tries to fully understand her own place as a woman in Islam. Tuzeen reads the *Qur'an* in Arabic with an accompanying translation in Urdu, and she reads the *hadith*. Reading texts provides Tuzeen with information, but the act of reading itself is also part of performing Muslim identity. As Homi Bhabha writes about identity, which is "signified in the process of repetition" (1994c, 53), a performance. Her identity as a Muslim woman is a series of performances and enactments of a particular way of being in the world. At the moment of reading the *Qur'an*, she is enacting her identity through the act of reading. And when asked about some of the things she does as a Muslim, she said:

> Tuzeen: I recite the *Qur'an* every day. I try to read the translation, and I try to understand it. If I don't understand, I will probably go into the Sunnah, but right now . . . there are lots of things my mind will not accept.

Tuzeen looks to religious texts for a more comprehensive understanding of women's rights and roles in Islam. She finds sexism in the *Qur'an* and in the Sunnah impossible to accept.

> Tuzeen: Like one ridiculous *hadith* . . . in *Sahih Bukhari* where it says that if you will not read your morning prayer, *Shaitan* [the devil] will be in your ear. To me, you can say those things to a child, [but] it does not make sense to me at all.

Tuzeen finds Bukhari's words paternalistic and not relevant to her as an adult woman: "Again this morning I read the whole *Sura Nisa,* and it said that men are above women. It is very clear, but my mind does not accept it." The verse Tuzeen particularly refuses to accept clearly states, "Men are maintainers of women, because Allah has made some of them to excel over others and because they spend out of their wealth."[7]

> Tuzeen: What about the cases where they [men] don't provide for women? I mean I have been working for the last twenty years, and obviously I have been providing for myself. That is why there is so much controversy about this same sentence. . . . It is hard for me to accept because I [have been] working for the last twenty years. . . . When I go deep into that, I am a little bit more inclined towards women's lib, not in the sense that it exists here. But I do think that women are equal.

Despite verses in the *Qur'an* that suggest inequality, Tuzeen's claims for equality with men arise from a reading of the sacred texts that challenges historical readings which reinforce the subordination of women in Muslim societies and communities.

> Shahnaz: In what way are women equal to men in Islam?

> Tuzeen: I don't go into any details. I follow the basic religion, which is *iman* [faith], *zakat* [charity], *salat* [prayer], fasting, hajj [pilgrimage to Mecca].

Tuzeen does not accept certain statements that point to the unequal status of women in Islam, and she truly believes that Muslim women can be equal to men. This equality does not always prevail because many women do not read the religious texts to decide for themselves what to accept. She says that she reads and tries to understand the meaning and then decides not only what to accept into her daily life but also what the rights and responsibilities of men should be. Quoting the sura that gives men the right to more than one wife,[8] Tuzeen then points out:

> Men are abusing the religion. They are using the first part for their own advantage, and they are not using the second part because they don't want to do that. So it is men's mistake, not religion's. And it makes me angry. That is where women have to be educated and where women have to stand up . . . and demand their rights. And I really believe that the rights women have been given by religion are good.

Tuzeen realizes that there is a difference in how the message of equality gets lived out between Muslim women and men here and those in Pakistan. Of her relationship with her husband she says, "we are equal," even though she believes that equality may not have been possible had they been living in Pakistan. This could be, she claims, because the dynamics of their relationship developed outside of the influence of family, particularly in-laws.

Tuzeen had not heard about the movement to have *Shari'a* in Canada. When I pointed it out to her, she thought *Shari'a* to be alright for those who wanted to follow it.

> Tuzeen: *Shari'a* law is okay if somebody wants to follow it. What do you mean, they want to have *Shari'a* in Canada? For everyone?

> Shahnaz: For consenting Muslims, because they are saying you cannot be Muslim unless you are following the *Shari'a* laws.

> Tuzeen: Which *Shari'a* laws? There are so many. I don't know. . . . I will read what they want to say in *Shari'a*, what they really mean, before I accept it. I will not accept it just like that.

Her choice of the words "really mean" seems to suggest that although *Shari'a* is divine, the application is not and can be challenged through reading and education. She pointed out that *Shari'a* puts more responsibility on male members of the family than on the female members: "My brother is responsible for my mother and for my unmarried sister, while I am not."

For Tuzeen the central role for the Muslim woman is that of the Muslim mother:

> Tuzeen: Women have the most important job, [one] that men do not have. That is why [the] *Qur'an* has given women so much respect. That job is bringing up children; that means bringing up the culture. . . .

Women get involved in professional positions where they have to work twelve hours a day, and they come home tired [and] cannot look after the children. They are with the maids and whoever is looking after the children. Society deteriorates. I think there is nothing, nothing more important, more respectful from my point of view, and I think from religious point of view, than to bring up a child.

Tuzeen's statements reinforce the role of the Muslim woman as the guardian of identity and culture. Yet such women "are honoured as long as they keep culture and religion in the way they are meant to; breeders and raisers of good Muslims" (Helie-Lucas 1994, 394). Tuzeen's situation is such that she has the support of her husband and the majority of her own family. Thus, despite her nonacceptance of certain aspects of the religious texts, she has been able to fulfil her role as the Muslim mother and wife.

For Tuzeen, Islam is important, not only spiritually but also as an identity. She is clear about this identity. The structural contradictions in the Muslim woman's identity do not pose a problem for her. She rejects many of the sexist interpretations and practices as well as the stereotypes. She does her own research and decides what she will accept, and she accepts that which seemingly gives her agency and empowers her. As a hybridized subject Tuzeen challenges prescriptions of authority in her daily life. She initiates new codes and signifiers that allow her to come to terms with the unequal status of woman in the sacred. At the same time the sacred provides her with spiritual strength and stability as she creates her space as a reflective and creative Muslim minority female in Canada.

Donna

Being Muslim in Canada means being different, devalued, and categorized into multicultural communities. How is this difference defined? For the women whose narratives have been discussed so far, race and Islamic cultural identities position them as different through embodiment, dress, customs, and rituals. As these thirteen women confront the meaning of Muslim womanhood, they have to figure out how they are going to negotiate the myriad networks they are involved in within their families. Donna is different. Her mother was Maltese, and her father was of Scottish descent. Donna was born a Catholic in Malta in 1950 but has since converted to Islam.[9] As a white woman, she can draw on a reservoir of what Peggy McIntosh (1990) calls unearned white privilege. Yet she has chosen Islam, by virtue of which she will be somewhat outside this privilege. Thus Donna's conversion to Islam positions her uniquely with respect to the Muslim woman. She is white and the member of the "privileged group" as well as the "Other" by virtue of being Muslim.

Donna came to Canada with her parents when she was seven years old. She attended a Catholic school in Toronto, an experience she remembers as being in a sheltered environment. Other children were also from a Catholic immigrant background.

> Donna: When I got out of that sheltered environment of high school and went to college, I was like blown away by the difference. . . . I felt like the rug was pulled right from under me, and I went flying, and I did everything that everybody else in college was doing, maybe in a limited way. . . . I did drugs. I got into sex. . . .

She went to church on Sundays while she was at home but stopped when she moved out. She married a man of Scottish background and had a daughter. Her husband was an alcoholic, and the eight years she was married to him she says were focused on survival in an abusive relationship. She finally left him in 1983. At this point, she bought into the consumerism of Canadian society: the clothes, the makeup, and the men.

> Donna: It was awful because I really didn't know who I was, and so I was playing at being somebody. But I really didn't know that I was playing at being somebody, so I couldn't really understand this confusion and the unhappiness. Why am I not happy? I mean I am enjoying the sex. I am enjoying this; I am enjoying that. I was very discreet. I never brought men into the house. I was aware that was not the image that I wanted my daughter to have of men, but I wanted that image for myself somehow. It was very strange.

She says she realized that sexual freedom has been used to exploit women sexually by men who are not willing to make a commitment or to take responsibility.

A few years ago she took a course at a community college where she had to do inner searching in a group setting. She found the process interesting because she was one of the few people in the course who was not Canadian-born. In this course she realized that she approached things in a generally different way than the "average" Canadian, whom Donna identifies as someone who is born here.

At this time, Donna started to work for a refugee organization and again realized that she had more in common with newcomers to Canada than with her "Canadian friends."

> Donna: Just the way these people socialize, the way they are, their manners . . . their feeling of concern for each other. They are close with family.

Donna started dating an Iranian man and was impressed by his commitment to a religion, Islam, which she had thought was very sexist. She became curious and started reading up on Islam and particularly women's rights in Islam. She got more and more interested and began to think about converting. About the time she was making up her mind, she recalls going to a bar with some friends:

> Donna: This one guy got drunker and drunker, and in the end he couldn't hold his head up, and he ended up with his face on the table filled with beer and stains of beer. And I am sitting there beside this guy, and I am thinking, "What am I doing here? Is this how I want to spend the rest of my life, partying? You know, this is not fun any more. Okay, dancing is fun, but sitting here in this place with cigarettes and smell of beer and some guy almost throwing up beside me, this is not fun."

Donna's account suggests a connection between being Muslim and not drinking alcohol, thus discounting everyday practices of millions of Muslims around the world, many of whom are alcoholics. Nevertheless, Donna talked to people, read books, and talked at length to a member of the Islamic community (who was also a convert) about women's rights, polygamy, wearing the *hejab,* and about all the things that struck her about Islam. It took her a year to decide to convert. She was getting to the point of thinking:

> Donna: Why am I reading all this stuff? Is it because I want to do it or what? You know, I was getting so involved with it that it was sort of pointless carrying on reading without becoming [Muslim]. It was the only way of really experiencing it all.

She recalls: "I was reading this English version of *Qur'an.* There were things in the *Qur'an,* some words that came right off the page and hit me, and I know that sounds very weird." She converted to Islam in the spring of 1988 and is now married to a Moroccan. At the time of this interview she was expecting their first child.

Since Donna was raised a Catholic, she claims that she did not have a ready-made cultural "springboard" from which to define her difference as a Muslim. Donna's skin color does not differentiate her from what she considers the "average Canadian." She commented that because I am darker than she is, my difference is visible. I do not have to define it, she says, while she feels the need to do so. For Donna, being a white woman was a hindrance in her search for identity as a Muslim woman. Clearly Donna sees this identity as an othered identity. And she says: "I am white, and I don't have an accent, though I have dark hair. I have never really stuck out like a visible minority."

Donna needs to have clear definition of her difference as a Muslim woman but had great difficulty in singling out "the authentic Muslim woman" to emulate culturally. For the first year and a half after her conversion to Islam she was not sure what being Muslim entailed:

Shahnaz: When you converted to Islam, what did you feel you had to do to be Muslim?

Donna: This is where my confusion started. . . . The majority of people who are Muslim are non-Western or their parents were, so they have background from some Muslim country. Malta is not a Muslim country, so I couldn't identify with [the] Maltese in the same way. And I knew that I wasn't Pakistani, and I wasn't from an African country. I didn't know how to dress, and I didn't know how to speak properly in Islamic terms. I didn't know any of this stuff, so I got confused. I was in agony for about the first year and a half of being a Muslim because I didn't know how to dress properly. That was a big thing for me. You know, all those people were all telling me different things. Once you become a Muslim, everybody wants to help you become a Muslim, everybody in the community.

Shahnaz: Which community?

Donna: Individuals in different communities. And individuals come from their own school of thought, and they say "You have to do this," and "You shouldn't be doing it that way," and "Your hair should be stuck under your scarf."

Shahnaz: The Qur'an says modest dress.

Donna: Exactly, exactly. That is one thing. But then when you read the Qur'an and it says you have to be covered from here to here . . . so I said, "Okay, fine." I started wearing long sleeves.

Shahnaz: But you are not wearing long sleeves now.

Donna: I am wearing a jacket, and if I didn't wear it, then I would have long sleeves on.

Shahnaz: So long sleeves is for outside?

Donna: Oh, yes. Around women I will wear shorter sleeves.

Shahnaz: I notice that you are not wearing a scarf.

Donna: . . . I guess one of my big problems—and this is where the scarf issue comes in—is that I don't really like to stick out in a crowd or anything.

Shahnaz: So you are not wearing a scarf partly because of what it will be like to walk down the street wearing a scarf?

Donna: Yes, yes. And I don't know how I could deal with that. It is not something to do with the scarf. . . . Now I look pretty well the same as everybody else. . . . I don't know where this comes from or why I am like that. . . . I would like to be more independent. . . . I would like to do what I want to do really.

Shahnaz: But you haven't reached that.

Donna: No, but maybe one day.

Donna wants to identify herself as different. Although she claims she does not know where her hesitancy comes from, her remarks suggest that she is aware of the negative reaction to veiled women, and she wants no part of it. Yet by focusing on dress as an inherent part of being a Muslim, Donna appears to be conflating intellectual and religious issues with the dress code. Perhaps this is because in popular mythology a large aspect of the Muslim difference is centered around notions of dress. Through consciously inserting herself into the existing notions of difference, Donna, a white woman, wants to enter the social and material reality of the outsider, the "Other," the Muslim woman. At the same time, she does not want to wear the *hejab,* as she does not appear to want the markings of ultimate otherness.

Perhaps Donna's difficulties lie in the very nature of her quest for an essentialized Muslim womanhood. Although in conventional wisdom there is a monolithic Islam and a single vision of the Muslim woman, in reality there is no single cultural Islam to emulate. The *Umma* is not a monolithic body. It consists of many diverse racial and cultural groups. Although the main Islamic texts, the *Qur'an* and the *hadith* literature, are the same for all groups, interpretations and forms of prescribed behavior as well as modes of dress tend to vary across regions. As such there are many determinations of dress for Muslim women. With so many competing visions of authenticity to chose from, Donna faces a dilemma that women who grew up in a Muslim family and in a Muslim country do not face.

Shahnaz: What does being Muslim mean to you?

Donna: . . . When I say Muslim I think of religion. . . . There are certain rules about being a part of a religion.

Shahnaz: Not everybody follows all the rules. Some of us follow some rules; some follow other rules.

Donna: Then why be part of a religion?

Shahnaz: For me being a Muslim, religion is a small part of it. The rest is the art, the culture, the history, the getting up hearing the *azzan,* the fasting in Ramadan—that is being a Muslim. I grew up with that.

Donna: Yes, but . . . having converted to Islam . . . I have to look for those things that are in Islam that isn't [sic] part of my culture, that is [sic] not part of my upbringing. And I am not going to find it like you did. I am not going to find it like anyone from a Muslim country is ever going to find it. I am never going to find it.

As she constructs herself as a Muslim woman, she does not have the resources of a family history of Islam. In a sense she is the flip side of Safieh. Safieh rejected the spirituality of Islam but cannot escape being connected to how Islamic female identity is constructed because she lives within Iranian/Muslim social networks. Donna has embraced the spirituality but does not have the historical and the sociological influences, so she has to rely on the sacred and use it to provide a model for her life. She constructs and enacts her identity as a Muslim woman based on religious and sociocultural texts. Donna's construction of herself as a Muslim focused heavily on prescriptions, substantiating Nabia's claim that a religious identity is all there is for Muslims in Canada.

Donna has looked to Islam for moral guidance. Her encounter with the institution of *muta* symbolized for her how men have manipulated religion for their own ends. Before she decided to convert to Islam, Donna was introduced to *muta* by an Iranian boyfriend.

Donna: This is how we ended up having sex, because he couldn't have sex without that. . . . I was really impressed with this. . . . I said, "My God, this guy is really serious." . . . You know, he is taking responsibility.

However, Donna read up on the subject and realized that he was doing *muta* because he was not going to marry her.

Donna: I have read a lot about it . . . and there are rules and regulations in *muta*. . . . I realized he wasn't doing even what his own Shia religion said about it, so I said "Wait a second." . . . I realized that the reason why he had *muta* marriage with me was because he wasn't ever going to really marry me. . . . Basically he said that in the beginning, but I thought that he is new here, and who knows what could happen in the future. I had thought that by somehow doing that [*muta*] he was being more responsible and generally we were okay together. We were responsible in terms of financially living together. When we were together, he would often eat at our place. He would provide grocery money; he would provide gas for the car. There was never any issue about that with him. My ex-husband was just horrible about money, and so I was impressed about all this. This guy is very responsible and all that, but he was looking for a younger woman. . . . Eventually I found out where the mosque was, and I had gone to get some information about that [*muta*], and I spoke to the Imam.

As Shahla Haeri (1989) points out, within the religious/cultural framework, the purpose of *nikah* (permanent marriage) is procreation, while that of *muta* is sexual enjoyment of the man and financial reward for the woman. Such a view denies the sexual feelings of women. Donna is not Shia, but her Iranian boyfriend was, and *muta* appears to be the only available means of having sex for those Shia Muslims who have accepted conventional rituals of identity. Although initially impressed, Donna now realizes the exploitation of women in the institution of *muta*, as well as the stigma attached to the temporary wife.

Like the majority of the women interviewed for this study, Donna gives a central role to Muslim mothering for the Muslim woman. This role creates a particular dilemma. Since her conversion, Donna has believed that the role of the Muslim mother is essential. Yet her daughter does not share her views:

> Donna: My daughter didn't convert. . . . She is not a Muslim. It has been a little bit difficult there because I have ideas of how I want her to be . . . in terms of her behavior. . . . If I was a Muslim when she was born, I would have raised her differently. . . . instead of [as] a nonreligious kind of person.
>
> Shahnaz: So this raises issues for you?
>
> Donna: This is my dilemma. My daughter is going out with guys. It has become a dilemma since I have become a Muslim and also since I started realizing what could go wrong for her if she isn't careful about herself. . . . But the other dilemma for me besides the safety is the spiritual side—she is totally an aspiritual child. She is not even sure that she believes in God. Can you imagine? . . . Other Muslims have told me, "Don't pressure her; she wasn't born Muslim. She grew up most of her life in a non-Muslim house." But you know it is hard. Islam says this and this about abortion, about birth control, and you have to inform your kids about it.

Donna says that the child she and her Moroccan-born husband are expecting will be raised as a Muslim. This child will have access to a Moroccan Muslim tradition and will be brought up within notions of authenticity inspired by Moroccan culture.

> Shahnaz: What are you thinking for the future? More understanding of Islam for yourself and your children?
>
> Donna: Yes, for myself, but not for my daughter. She has to choose her own way. For the child that I am going to have . . . the father is Muslim

and comes from a Muslim country. He would have to do a lot of the guidance in terms of daily living. I mean I have a lot more understanding than before, but he would be guiding that child a lot more than I would in some ways. I would like to have an Islamic kind of family life where you celebrate the *Eid* and do all that stuff in Ramadan and do all the day-to-day stuff which I haven't had much experience with.

Donna's search for guidance regarding dress, ways of thinking, as well as acceptable behavior, led her to religious texts and also texts that critique sexism in Islam. Although Donna advocates the idea that Muslim women can and should come together and form a common front against sexism in Islamic practices, she notes that feminist perspectives of Islam, including those that view Muslim women in bondage to their husbands, are wrong and narrow.

Shahnaz: This something which many women writers are also complaining about, for instance Fatima Mernissi and Leila Ahmed.

Donna: I disagree with those women [Mernissi and Ahmed] who are fighting those issues. I fight those issues too. . . . My God, I work in a women's shelter, and I know what a lot of Muslim men are doing. But in this case women who are fighting for rights will say that Islam is the cause of that [women's oppression]. . . . I believe you can fight it, and quite Islamicly you can fight those issues. There is a lot in Islam that will uphold women's rights.

Donna has read Mernissi's *Beyond the Veil* (1987), and she says she does not agree with the message in Mernissi's work that religion holds women back. She also expressed concerns about the work of Ahmed, a Muslim feminist cultural theorist (1982, 1992), who, she claims, questions sexism in the sacred texts. She believes that concerns of sexism in the sacred should be directed at male interpretations instead of the religious texts themselves.

Donna has embraced Islam as an egalitarian religion, which she says has been misinterpreted:

Donna: . . . My husband told me that the way many people translate the *Qur'an* is wrong. . . . I don't even know for sure about some of the authenticity of translations. When we are blaming Islam, should we not be blaming these guys that are writing history?

Shahnaz: Many women are doing that. Many women are questioning the translations and the inscriptions as well as the selective use of texts to form policy and law.

Donna: Exactly, exactly, and they [policy and law makers] don't emphasize the ones about what men have to do. What men's responsibilities are. And one imam actually said to the men, he said, "Look, you gave up your responsibilities. What do you expect? You cannot ask for rights from your wife if you give up your responsibilities."

Selective usage and interpretations of Islamic texts by men, Donna believes, do not address the issues that come up for women in their daily lives. A lack of attention in Canada to women's issues by community leaders, she believes, will cause Muslim women to opt for secular solutions, which she sees as undesirable.

Donna is also concerned with the stereotypes of the Muslim women that individual Muslim women confront, particularly in women's shelters. She has worked at several shelters and is aware of the contradictions present in them. On one hand, they provide refuge to abused Muslim women, but, on the other hand, staff (white and nonwhite) have biases against Islam and Muslims. At a shelter she visited, she found the staff had teased an Arab woman into taking off her *gellabeyya* and was on the point of getting her to take off her scarf when Donna intervened.[10]

> Donna: . . . This is happening in shelters in many places. There is this idea that you have to liberate those women. There is no thought about what this is going to do to them. You send them out of the shelter alone, and you take every support system away from them.

Here Donna voices a concern similar to Zahra's and that mosque officials also expressed to me. The priority at shelters is to find solutions outside family and culture. Donna also had concerns about the insensitivity around dietary requirements.

> Donna: If you have a woman and her kids in there, and they are used to eating *halal* meat and they can't eat any other meat, like if you are serving pork, they can't eat it. . . . The shelters, some of them just won't . . . even make the attempt to do so. They might buy kosher meat. . . . One woman in the shelter told me that the staff sort of made her feel guilty about her child not having meat because it was not *halal*. . . . You know that it is not fair to not let the child have it.

Donna does not believe in the centrality of *Shari'a* for Muslims, as she realizes that it involves a sexist interpretation of religious texts. As for having *Shari'a* in Canada: "I am really against it. I read a report . . . by that group who had sponsored it, and I was like, 'Please, God, don't let this happen'." She is concerned about which version of *Shari'a* will be promoted and how it is going to affect women. Donna has no qualms about calling it sexist and misogynist.

As a convert, Donna is invested in Islam as the best blueprint for spiritual and secular life. Yet her narrative suggests that she never accepts

Islamic interpretations, as she calls them, without question. Her view of Muslim female empowerment suggests incorporating progressive interpretations of the sacred into strategies of resistance. She reads material on the roles and options available to women in Islam. She takes inspiration from what she calls the "basic message" of the texts and discards the rest as sexist interpretation.

> Donna: I like being a Muslim, and I don't see that it is a problem being a Muslim and being a woman, being an independent, thoughtful woman and making [my] own decisions. I wish people would [understand]. I mean I was there, too, so I know why people are thinking that way, but I wish that people would sort of get that [stereotypes] out of their heads.

Donna's negotiations and translations attest to her positioning as a hybridized subject in the third space. She rejects the sexism in Islamic prescriptions as well as the stereotypes of Muslim women. Donna enacts her Muslim female identity, an identity of resistance and collusion as she reads anew the sacred and makes sense of it in her life as an independent, reflective woman.

Conclusion

Ethnicity often comes packaged with a sense of authenticity attributed to minority cultures, "alien" religions, or "mother tongues" and is associated with an exotic otherness, which simultaneously attracts and repels. Frequently there is also a conflation of ethnicity and identity, while the centrality of the white, Anglo culture in North America remains unquestioned. Within multicultural paradigms ethnicity is also categorized and racialized into "different" cultural communities. Multicultural policy and practices frequently support discursive articulations of community as static. In particular, assumptions of a monolithic patriarchal Muslim community assert a strong presence in popular North American imagination.

Recent trends in cultural politics have challenged conventional determinations of ethnicity, identity, and community by emphasizing hybridity and diaspora rather than roots, authenticity, and homogeneity as central themes. In particular, these trends have been articulated in the work of cultural theorists such as Homi Bhabha, Gayatri Spivak, Avtar Brah, Stuart Hall, and Ali Rattansi. Whether their work suggests linguistically or materially based dynamic notions of identity, their analyses shift away from narrow identity politics determined by static or essentialized notions of race, gender, and class and toward a rearticulated politics of difference. In particular, Rattansi argues for a definition of culture that is no longer limited to religious beliefs, communal rituals, and shared traditions but instead understands culture as a process and knowledge "through which particular communities are defined" (1992a, 4). This politics recognizes structures of inequality and discrimination but contests them through a mobile and shifting strategy of representation and association, encompassing diverse perspectives and experiences.

Current immigration patterns suggest that many different and diverse racialized groups are making their homes in North America. Engagement between groups through preconceived notions of difference is a trap that is well worth avoiding. It is crucial that cultural and racial difference not be understood as the free play of polarities of us and them. It would be useful instead to suggest that the contradictory negotiations of a hybridized identity open up a third space where cultural allegiances are the "site of an ambivalent identification; a margin of the uncertainty of cultural meaning that may become the space of an agonistic minority position" (Bhabha 1994c, 167). One possibility is a move away from the authentic and toward hybridity and a rescripting of codes and categories within a third space. The idea of hybridity and the third space identifies the mixing that occurs in urban space in contemporary diasporic communities. The hybridized site is similar to the double bind in the sense that both are positioned at the intersection of contradiction and ambivalence. Yet to be in a double bind can mean not only being immobilized by the binaries, the polarities, and the stereotypes but also being vulnerable to cultural relativist demands. Bhabha's notion of hybridity, on the other hand, moves away from overdetermined subjectivity to a creative critical space that emphasizes neither one polarity nor the other and refuses to reduce one binary to the other. And as Bhabha and others suggest, this third space allows for progressive politics and resistance. The diasporic mixing in the third space is not about temporary sojournment but about putting roots elsewhere. Brah reminds us that "[although] the word diaspora often invokes the imagery of traumas of separation and dislocation . . . diasporas are also potentially sites of hopes and new beginnings. They are contested cultural and political terrains, where individual and collective memories collide, reassemble and reconfigure" (1996, 193).

I want to dislodge ethnicity from identity and decenter it as well. I want to critique the established notion and practice of "community," but at the same time I do not want to valorize the individual subject. Instead I want to highlight the highly complex and contradictory ways that negotiations in the form of resistance and collusion occur between the individual and communities.

Males and females alike at times hold patriarchal visions of "community," and frequently these visions are at odds with the many contradictory and heterogeneous opinions within various communities. I want to reinforce this process of social imaginary as a Muslim woman's third space. This third space both emerges from the dynamic notion of culture and also gives rise to it. It is a space in which Lourdes Torres's analysis (1991) of Latina cultural and gender socialization and misinformation in the United States can be situated. Static and binary discourses and practices, Torres points out, have left women with contradictory and fragmented identities. The radical and progressive negotiation of this fragmented self, Torres believes, is the refusal to accept one position. Donna Harraway (1990) has also pointed to the notion of fractured, contradictory identities, which are partial and strategic. She proposes exploring fully politicized identities of oppositional consciousness and coalition. I find the idea of a politicized, creative, in-between, fluid space very appealing. Yet within such a mobile determination of identity the very act of naming poses a danger of exclusion. In the freezing of categories, even within progressive political articulations, there will be those who do not get named. While the exclusionary effects of this naming can never be totally mitigated, a productive tension can be maintained between desire for fluidity and the process of naming. This productive space can fuel projects of possibility. Through creative engagement with the regulating influences of their lives, the fourteen women in this book attest to the hybridized identities formed in the third space in contemporary North America.

As Brah suggests, "All diasporas are differentiated, heterogeneous, contested spaces, even as they are implicated in the construction of a common "we" (1996, 184). Hybrid negotiations remind us that postcolonial history happens not only outside North America but also within. This history of the colonial "adventure" and its continuing aftereffects, so traumatic for its victims, have been consistently disavowed and distorted in the combined knowledge and memory of colonizing Euro-Americans. As diasporic peoples come and settle or sojourn in North America, displaced narratives of postcolonial peoples (immigrants, refugees, and permit holders, as well as those silent and uncounted who have no legal status, such as migrant workers and illegal aliens) increasingly demand a social and political presence. The holism of Western history found in the liberal canon is disrupted in the Muslim woman's third space, reversing the effects of colonial disavowal by allowing denied and distorted knowledge into the popular imagination. Inclusion of disavowed knowledge moves us away from notions of the originary and authentic and unsettles the cultural relativist position from which notions of "traditional community" draw strength. Exploring the community as heterogeneous and contradictory complicates the singular vision of culture, allowing for notions of uncertain, shifting cultural meaning as hybridized sites of Muslim identity. The ambivalence of women's lives can then be recognized through this prism, and the sites of resistance can be identified.

Although the notion of third space could lend itself to many projects of possibility for marginalized ethnicities, sexualities, and oppositional locations, I have used it in connection with a Muslim woman third space. In this redefinition I do not mean to propose that each ethnic racial group of women would construct a "third space" specific to their own positioning. Rather, I want to explore the myriad of possibilities that open up within a third space for differently positioned Muslim women.

The narratives discussed in this book are testimony that these women are attempting to constitute a third space in which they receive recognition as Muslim at the same time they are contesting the regulatory pressures of the Orientalist stereotypes and fundamentalist-influenced mythology of the *Umma*. Some of the accounts convey depression and hopelessness, and these emotions frequently arise out of a sense of not living up to pre-established notions of Muslim identity. The narratives suggest that these women are not passively receiving Islamic or dominant cultural practices but are actively engaging with their circumstances in complex and contradictory ways. The women's marginalization by racist, sexist, and religious discourses leads them to reject prescriptions of authenticity. Although none of the women is connected to a fundamentalist or Islamist context, their narratives to some extent promote an Orientalist conflation of Islam and Islamism. Yet they also negotiate dynamic identities of collusion, resistance, and contestation.

The women's narratives indicate that in their daily negotiations they initiate new signifiers and symbols of identities as they forge novel possibilities by defying prescriptions and expectations. In opening up supplementary discourses, they rescript the originary through individual and collaborative strategies of resistance, contestation, and collaboration in the process of cultural, political, and economic empowerment in Canada. Their empowerment, which is on the frontiers of the dominant culture, opens up a third space as a hybridized site of Muslim female identity in Canada. This notion of Muslim female identity does not depend on pregiven traits of tradition at "home." Rather, it is a complex negotiation that depends on consensus as much as conflict, and religion and tradition are only partial aspects of the contradictory nature of women's lives.

The word *Muslim* suggests a collective identity, a master narrative, a myth of the *Umma*, and the exotic/barbaric Other. A Muslim feminist thus becomes a contradiction. Shahrzad Mojab (1995) speaks of this contradiction but, in not moving beyond the religious paradigm, inadvertently her argument reinforces the notion of religion as being the only issue for Muslims. In my use of the words *Muslim feminist*, I would prefer to make reference to an historical, patriarchal collective, which is enticing to some women. Yet women also express a desire for agency within the collective and for woman-centered political alliances either as individuals and/or as members of the collective. A contradictory position! These contradictions are embedded in the dynamic, unstable, and forever changing hybridized third space women inhabit, which cannot be contained in the familiar static discourses and arguments through which the Muslim woman is normally articulated.

A rescripting of the Muslim woman might accompany rules of recognition that reflect the complex and contradictory notion of hybridized identity. Unitary references to race, religion, and culture, which preserve the primacy of tradition and thus patriarchy, need constantly to be questioned. I argue that progressive scholarship and practice continue to reinforce a splitting within the binary poles of Orientalism and Islamism. Orientalism/West could conceivably continue to split into racist stereotypes about the Muslim "Other" and the right for women to become active agents. Historicizing racist discourses, particularly those that emphasize modernity, allows a view of cultures and civilizations as interconnected. Such a framework helps diffuse the rigid boundaries between Islam and the West and gives women the option of individual choice without being labeled anti-Islamic.

A discussion of women's complex negotiations needs to acknowledge two interconnected visions. First, the vision draws upon the strength of women who want to and/or have to incorporate religion into a strategy of women's empowerment. Progressive interpretations of the sacred, which are consciously more egalitarian but still acknowledge God's authority, are not legitimized within either Muslim societies or Muslim communities. Work that feminist scholars, such as Fatima Mernissi, Leila Ahmed, and Riffat Hassan, are doing to undermine the androcentric foundations of patriarchal interpretation of religious texts is crucial in this regard. The use of their work by Muslim women to establish legal precedents in Pakistan is one example of praxis of the theoretical within the political realm.[1]

The second vision acknowledges the group of women who want to and/or are able to work outside religious frameworks. Historically, there is little precedent for a clear separation between religion and the state in Islam. Thus, for the second group of visionaries, in view of the sexist nature of the interpretations that are legitimized, the conflation of "Islamic" and "Muslim" positions women so that any move toward equality becomes a questioning of divine authority. Under current conditions, where the influence of Islamism is increasing globally in conjunction with racist stereotypes about Muslims in the West, a splitting of Islamic into Islam, the religion, and Muslim, the person who lives a day-to-day reality, is one method of reinforcing women's empowerment. For those women who wish to and are able to work outside the religious frameworks, a separation of the sacred from the cultural will allow them to claim their social and political histories without being confined to religious prescriptions.[2]

The splitting of Orientalism and Islamism so identified is difficult to sustain in an everyday life in the Western metropolis, where women are racialized as Muslims and have to face increasing social and sexual control within their own communities and families, particularly since there is no established vision they can turn to for affirmation. Expressions of ambivalence occur because women are pulled in the different directions of Islamism and Orientalism by the splitting within the two continua. The struggle for agency and identity as a Muslim woman thus becomes a site of both affirmation and disorientation.

Opening up the third space allows me to position myself theoretically and politically in the contradictory liminal space of always becoming. I will no longer have to respond with my single timeless Muslim truth. Instead I can locate my Muslim identity as shifting and contradictory. It is a space that will have to be contested and where the concept of difference will have to be engaged with rather than suppressed.

In North America, this contested notion of Muslim womanhood creates a marginalizing, unsettling, diasporic experience like Bhabha's notion of hybridization, where subjects are formed "'in between,' or in excess of, the sum of the 'parts' of difference" (1994b, 269). It is an experience that begins with the location of the women in a context where culture and religion play an important but not defining part. Rather, culture and religion are stepping-stones through which other experiences such as gender, class, race, social and political location, and sexuality are mediated. In this way there is no return to an "original" past unmediated by the brutal horror of colonialism and the present circumstances of refugee experience, immigration, displacement, racialization, devaluation, exclusion, and exploitation in employment.

Through this discussion I have complicated the term *Muslim* in the hope of unsettling what the term evokes. In moving away from the notion of ascriptive identity based on predetermined religious or ethnic characteristics, I have engaged with the term *Muslim* as a process. My aim is to reinforce a political third space through which struggles against sexism and fundamentalism within diasporic communities or challenges to sexism at "home" will no longer fuel liberal racism. In particular, I want to connect representational practices with the local conditions in which women are positioned in diasporic societies. The image of the Muslim woman oppressed and encased in a shroud is one major filter through which I and other Muslim women mediate our subject positions in North America. I want to challenge the homogenization of Muslim women as well as the conflation of women living in Muslim societies and those in diasporic contexts, so that we move beyond stereotypes to an understanding of the local conditions that position women in specific and often unfortunate ways. Instead of blaming Muslim men for the conditions of Muslim women, Western feminists might seek collaboration with the progressive forces within Muslim communities and together imagine more productive and dynamic interventions.

The women's daily negotiations suggest a hybrid and dynamic notion of Muslim identity, a reality of the postmodern, postcolonial world. A challenge is posed for scholars and activists to view and engage with the Muslim difference that is not monolithic and homogenous. Instead we might imagine and engage with a more open notion of Muslim, informed not only by religion and notions of static stereotypical culture, but also by popular culture as the multiple sites of a shifting, contradictory, and dynamic identity. Perhaps we ought to reconsider Julie Stephens's (1989) proposal that feminism engage with all tensions that make up women's struggles. For those women who identify with or are codified by others as Muslim, the sites of struggle are never singular, but always plural, shifting, and dynamic.

Notions of stable identity repress internal heterogeneity and are negotiated against the excluded "different." The idea of stable identity promoted in many Muslim societies through nationalist, anticolonialist movements is currently under considerable pressure. War and economic and ecological disasters have precipitated migrations, displacements, dislocations, and diasporas of people and resulted in loss of community and networks of kinship. Communities are scattering to urban areas and to other countries, including First World nations, in search of work and a better life. Meanwhile, "Muslimness" as a narrow, seemingly stable, and consequently enticing identity is being promoted through various Islamist movements.

What I have been arguing is that Muslim identity is not waiting to be discovered in the pages of the sacred or in stereotypical descriptions. It is a history that has to be grasped through a deconstruction of the Orientalist gaze and a destabilizing of Islamist desire for a coherent Muslim identity. It emerges from women's narration of their lives, and their testimonies are not accounts of a history of dominance but subaltern, contradictory histories of collusion and resistance. Women's testimonies disrupt homogenizing fundamentalism, Orientalism, and liberal feminism and suggest that these frames are discursively situated. Women's hybridized identity then becomes a grounding space, not a final space. In this space identity is always in process of formation. And in this third space identity is always constructed through ambivalence and splitting—between self and other. As Stuart Hall points out in another context (1997), splitting between love and desire, desire for that part of ourself we love but want to expel as the Other. Desire for and a reclaiming of the Other break down barriers between self and other. This is what women's negotiations testify to, and this is the message of their struggles.

APPENDIX

TO WHOM IT MAY CONCERN

Dear Madam:

I am a student at OISE and currently doing research toward a Ph.D. My research seeks to explore the experiences of Muslim women living in Canada. In this regard I would like to ask you to complete the attached questionnaire and interview you about your experiences. Also, I would like your permission to tape the interview.

All proceedings connected with the interview will be kept strictly confidential under lock and key. Only those involved in the research will have access to the information. If names are used in my analysis, they will be fictionalized.

Your participation in the research is voluntary, and you may withdraw it at any time you wish. Your support would be greatly appreciated.

       Yours sincerely,
       Shahnaz Khan

I consent to participate in the research.

NAME: _____ DATE:_____

ADDRESS: _____

TELEPHONE: _____

QUESTIONNAIRE

1. Are you a first-generation immigrant in Canada? If so:

a. number of people in your household in the country you came from:

_____

b. number of people in your household in Canada: _____

2. If you are not a first-generation immigrant in Canada:

a. number of people in the household you grew up in: _____

b. number of people in the household you are currently living in:

_____

3. How many years of schooling do you have? _____

How many were obtained in Canada? _____

4. Are you employed? _____

If yes, how many interviews did you have before you got the job?

_____

5. If you are not employed, are you looking for work? _____

If yes, how long have you been looking for work? _____

NOTES

Introduction

1. Homi Bhabha's notions of third space and hybridity will be developed throughout this manuscript.

2. Members of migrant communities are to an extent rearticulated through the politics of the spaces that are made available to minorities in the West. In particular, the North American context frequently generates two very different but reductionist views of Muslims: an Orientalist dismissal of the Muslim Other together with an overdetermining Islamic doctrine that limits the parameters in which a woman may identify herself or function as Muslim. I have previously examined these ideas elsewhere (Khan 1995c) and will further elaborate on them in this book.

3. For a discussion of a proposed parallel system that would bring in *Shari'a* for Muslims living in Canada, see Khan 1993.

4. In using linguistic expressions such as *dialogue* and *conversation,* I invoke Stuart Hall's ideas that the discursive and ideological are structural and have very material effects on our everyday lives. See Grossberg 1996.

Chapter 1. Negotiating the Third Space

1. Benedict Anderson (1983) has argued persuasively for the narrative of the Western nation to be understood as written in homogenous serial time.

2. The image of self is negative and at some level encourages a disavowal of the self as seen through those devalued attributes.

3. See Julia Clancy Smith 1992.

4. Notable among Western scholars who conducted serious inquiry with integrity are Louis Massignon, Maxine Rodinson, and the English scholar H. A. R. Gibb; Gibb left Oxford to become professor of Arabic at Harvard in 1955.

5. I refer to the connections that Chatterjee (1986) has made between nationalist thought in India and the discourse of Orientalism to help explore the desire of a generic feminism of Egyptian women at the turn of the century.

6. Although white, this original cannot be collapsed into white as the power group, as there are many "different" minority positions within the notion of white, for example, French, Italian, Irish, etc. Also, many groups of white people with

alternative lifestyles, such as gays and lesbians, form their own subcultures within the larger white paradigm. See Dyer 1997. As the majority of Muslims are visible minorities, however, my interest rests with visible minorities.

7. Fanon (1967) and Bhabha (1994c), among others, have explored the contradictory relationship between the colonized and the colonial stereotypes and the ways in which the colonized also turn away from these stereotypes about themselves. See note 9 below.

8. For a discussion of Orientalist construction of Muslim women, see Mabro 1991, Kabani 1986, Alloula 1986, and Lazreg 1990.

9. The colonial stereotype, along with notions of a structured condition of ambivalence and simultaneous alienation, is central to Homi Bhabha's construction of the colonial subject in discourse. The colonial stereotype, Bhabha states, is a source of attraction (in that the colonial subject recognizes her/himself) and a source of aversion (in that the colonial subject turns away from her/himself). Simultaneous alienation thus occurs at the nexus of desire and aversion, at a point when both the colonized and the colonizer turn away from the stereotype (Bhabha 1990a).

Chapter 2. Subjects of Study

1. The word *Shia* means sect. Shias are a minority in Islam, yet in Iran more than ninety percent of the people are Shia. There are also large minorities of Shias living in Iraq, Syria, and Lebanon.

2. A Muslim minority sect.

3. Sunnis make up ninety percent of Muslims. They are said to be followers of the Sunnah, or the path of the Prophet.

Chapter 3. Resolving the Contradictions through Disavowal

1. Interestingly, Karima's sons continue to feel the need to control their sisters in Canada. See chapter 4.

2. The *shalwar* and *kameez* are the basic trousers and long tunic of Pakistani dress, while the *dupatta,* or long scarf, is meant to cover the head and upper part of the body. Currently many women in Pakistan, particularly among the affluent classes, do not use it to cover their heads.

3. Wa Thiong'O Ngugi (1989) has argued that education in the colonial language breaks the harmony between school and home. The language of the culture and school are no longer one. Instead, the language of the school deliberately devalues indigenous culture. When those of us who have had such an education see ourselves through the rhetoric of the colonizers, a part of us continues to devalue another part of us. For instance, Indians and Pakistanis may see themselves through the eyes of Rudyard Kipling, Africans through Joseph Conrad, and Egyptians through Gustave Flaubert. Bhabha calls this phenomenon "the exercise of colonial power through discourse" (1990a, 72), which fosters notions of racial and sexual difference and produces an ambivalence in those so constructed. Such westernized educational systems, however, are expensive and available only to

people from a certain class. Because they are widely patronized by the elites of the "Third World," their institutionalization serves to deepen class separation.

4. Logically, a claim to represent ninety percent of Muslims would be difficult to support. Although there is no single Muslim Sunni community, the concept of such a community feeds into the stereotypical assumptions about the monolithic "Islamic community." Such views help reinforce and sustain racist determinations of Muslims and of Muslim women in particular. Although Zubaida is *Ahemdiyia* and as such belongs to a minority group, she is also Sunni.

5. Although the Ottoman Empire and Turkish Republic certainly experienced pressures from the West, Turkey was never colonized directly. Through changes initiated by Kemal Attaturk, the Turkish modernist reformer, since the early 1900s Turkey has moved from being the theological center of Islam and the seat of the caliphate toward a European identity. Turks, however, were negatively stereotyped in the first and last thirds of the twentieth century and then sank into oblivion in most American and Canadian minds, despite Turkish involvement in Cyprus. In Europe the situation is very different. Turkey has found little acceptance among the European community, as can be seen by the rejection of the Turkish application to join the European Economic Community and the increasing discrimination against the Turks in Germany. These moves have occurred in conjunction with growing Islamist pressures in Turkey.

6. Nikhat's responses reinforce the dichotomy of Europeans and Muslims as distinct categories and deny the existence of millions of Muslims in Europe.

Chapter 4. Negotiating the Ambivalence

1. Conventional wisdom deems that all Muslims are Arabs. Thus, as a South Asian, Iram would not be considered Muslim.

2. Many Muslim feminists refuse to abandon Muslim identity and struggle over what it means. This discussion is also an attempt to identify the complexities of Muslim identity.

3. Homosexuality is condemned in the *Qur'an* in references to the story of Lot and his followers. While directing that offenders be punished, the *Qur'an* does not specify the punishment. Forgiveness is offered to those who repent. See Greenberg 1984.

4. Hyderabad, in central India, had previously been ruled by a Muslim minority.

5. *Eid-ul-Fitr* and *Eid-ul-Azha* are the two Muslim feast days.

6. For an analysis of social, political, and sexual positioning of the colonial Indian woman, see McBratney 1988.

7. *Azan* is the call to prayer.

8. *Iftar* refers to the meal in the evening at the end of the fast in Ramadan.

9. *Zakat* is one of the basic tenets of Islam and refers to a percentage of wealth given to the needy.

10. For further reference, see Leila Ahmed 1992.

11. Egyptian society provides an example of struggle between Western and

indigenous cultures wherein issues of religion, class, and nationalism become interlinked with "the woman question." The lower-middle and lower classes were adversely affected by westernization, and their resistance has increasingly taken an anti-West, pro-Islamic stance. For an in-depth discussion of the political, economic, and social implications of these issues, see Leila Ahmed 1992. No doubt in the Egypt of the 1990s, any woman who is in a government or public position would have to account to Islamist notions of authenticity.

12. Such use of minority forums in the "multiculture" paradigm promotes liberal containment of difference without a political voice for minorities.

13. *Muta,* or temporary marriage, is legally sanctioned among the Twelver *Shi'ites* who live predominantly in Iran. It is based on a temporary marriage contract, in which a man and an unmarried woman decide how long they want to stay married to each other (from one hour to ninety-nine years) and how much money is to be given to the temporary wife. See Haeri 1989.

14. *Halal* refers to what is allowed. Islam requires that Muslims eat only *halal* meat, that is, meat from animals slaughtered according to religious prescriptions.

15. When I refer to women harassing other women, it is not my intention to contribute to homophobia. Instead I want to point to sexual harassment as an issue of power between white and nonwhite women.

16. *Purdah* refers to the institutionalized segregation, seclusion, and veiling of women in South Asia.

17. Although I talk about the colonial marginalization of religions other than Christianity, it is not my intention to overlook the exclusion and marginalization of those "Third World" people who have converted to Christianity.

18. A *burkha* is the Indian subcontinent's version of the veil. It is a head-to-toe covering, sometimes white and sometimes black.

19. An example can be seen in Eqbal Ahmed's 1992 article highlighting the case of noted Pakistani scholar and activist Akhtar Hameed Khan, who has had several *fatwas* issued against him for writing a fable deemed by conservatives to defame Ali, son-in-law of the Prophet.

20. Such views were quite evident in the criticism directed at Sunera Thobhani, a South Asian, when she became president of the National Action Committee on the Status of Women in 1993. Popular editorials claimed that as a new immigrant to Canada and a minority, she would be unable to understand or relate to the issues and concerns of the broad spectrum of Canadian women.

Chapter 5. Selecting What to Believe

1. But I believe that trend is changing. Women in Islamic countries who are currently turning to Islam for inspiration (and particularly those who join Islamist movements) often read the *Qur'an* and are quite aware of what is in it. For a discussion of this trend in Egypt, see El Guindi 1981.

2. It is true that Muslim women often keep their family names when they marry, but it is the name of their father, the patriarch. Manal does not acknowledge the institutional requirement that she take on her husband's name as an instance of

Muslim patriarchal practices being replaced in Canada by Euro-American patriarchal traditions.

3. The right to keep the matrimonial home is not an Islamic practice but is rather a right that Egyptian women won after a long and bitter feminist struggle. The law that gives women this right has recently been repealed by the Egyptian government in the wake of Islamist pressure.

4. Chapter 4, sura 34 in the *Qur'an* says, "As for those from whom you fear disobedience, admonish them and send them to beds apart them" (*Koran* 1983).

5. For arguments suggesting the centrality of *Shari'a* within Islamist movements, see Hunter, ed. 1988.

6. A verse in the *Qur'an* allows men to marry up to four women in certain circumstances. "Marry such women as seen good to you, two or three, or four, but if you fear that you will not do justice, then [marry] only one or that which your right hand possesses. This is more proper that you may not do injustice" (*Koran* 1983, 4:3).

7. Koran 1983, 4:34.

8. See note 6.

9. Although Donna is partially Maltese, she considers herself white and passes for white in Canada.

10. *Gellabeyya* is the long dress many Arabs, women as well as men, wear.

Conclusion

1. For a broader discussion of how women-centered interpretations of Islamic religious texts have informed and empowered women's struggles in Pakistan, see Mumtaz and Shaheed 1987.

2. By proposing a separation of the sacred and secular, I do not mean to imply that the sacred and secular are not interconnected in complex ways. Rather, I want to point to the distinction between oppositional struggles that use alternative interpretations of the sacred as a means of empowerment and those that do not.

BIBLIOGRAPHY

Abdo, Nahla. "Race, Gender, and Politics: The Struggle of Arab Women." In *And Still We Rise: Feminist Political Mobilizing in Contemporary Canada,* edited by Linda Carty, 73–100. Toronto: Women's Press, 1993.

Abraham, Nabeel. "Anti-Arab Racism and Violence in the United States." In *The Development of Arab-American Identity,* edited by Ernest McCarus, 155–214. Ann Arbor: University of Michigan Press, 1994.

———. "Arab-American Marginality: Myths and Praxis." In *Arab Americans: Continuity and Change,* edited by B. Abu-Laban and M. Suleiman, 17–43. Belmont, Mass.: Association of Arab-American University Graduates, 1989.

Abraham, Sameer. "Detroit's Arab-American Community." In *Arabs in the New World: Studies on Arab-American Communities,* edited by Sameer Abraham and Nabeel Abraham, 84–108. Detroit: Center for Urban Studies, Wayne State University, 1983.

Abraham, Sameer, and Nabeel Abraham, eds. *Arabs in the New World: Studies on Arab-American Communities.* Detroit: Center for Urban Studies, Wayne State University, 1983.

Ahmed, Eqbal. "Law Against Justice." *Dawn* (Karachi, Pakistan) 4 (October 1992): 4.

Ahmed, Leila. "Western Ethnocentrism and Perceptions of the Harem." *Feminist Studies* 8, no. 3 (fall 1982): 521–34.

———. *Women and Gender in Islam.* New Haven: Yale University Press, 1992.

Alexander, Meena. *The Shock of Arrival: Reflections on Post-Colonial Experience.* Boston: South End Press, 1996.

Al Faruqi, Isma'il Raji. "The Islamic Critique of the Status Quo of Muslim Society." In *The Islamic Impulse,* edited by Barbara Stowasser, 226–43. Washington, D.C.: Center for Contemporary Arab Studies, Georgetown University, 1987.

Ali, Yasmin. "Muslim Women and the Politics of Culture and Ethnicity in Northern England." In *Refusing Holy Orders,* edited by Gita Sahgal and Nira Yuval-Davis, 101–23. London: Virago, 1992.

Alloula, Malek. *The Colonial Harem.* Minneapolis: University of Minnesota Press, 1986.

Amin, Samir. *Eurocentrism.* New York: Monthly Review Press, 1989.

Anderson, Benedict. *Imagined Communities: Reflections on the Origin and Spread of Nationalism*. New York: Verso, 1983.

Anthias, Floya, and Nira Yuval-Davis. "Contextualizing Feminisms: Gender, Ethnic and Class Divisions." *Feminist Review* 15 (1983): 62–75.

Anzaldua, Gloria. *Borderlands*. San Francisco: Aunt Lute, 1987.

Asad, Talal. *Genealogies of Religion*. Baltimore: Johns Hopkins University Press, 1993.

Badran, Margot. *Feminists, Islam, and Nation: Genders and the Making of Modern Egypt*. Princeton: Princeton University Press, 1995.

Barth, Fredrik. Introduction. *Ethnic Groups and Boundaries*, edited by Fredrik Barth. Boston: Little, Brown, 1969.

Bassiouni, M. Cherif. "A Search for Islamic Criminal Justice: An Emerging Trend in Muslim States." In *The Islamic Impulse*, edited by Barbara Stowasser, 244–54. Washington, D.C.: Center for Contemporary Arab Studies, Georgetown University, 1987.

Bhabha, Homi. "DissemiNation: Time, Narrative, and the Margins of the Modern Nation." In *The Location of Culture*, by Homi Bhabha, 139–70. London: Routledge, 1994a.

———. "Frontline/Borderposts." In *Displacements: Cultural Identities in Question*, edited by A. Bammer, 269–72. Bloomington: Indiana University Press 1994b.

———. *The Location of Culture*. London: Routledge, 1994c.

———. "The Other Question: Difference, Discrimination and the Discourse of Colonialism." In *Out There: Marginalization and Contemporary Cultures*, edited by Russell Ferguson, Martha Gever, Trinh T. Minh-Ha, and Cornel West, 71–88. Cambridge, Mass.: MIT Press, 1990a.

———. "Signs Taken for Wonders: Questions of Ambivalence and Authority under a Tree outside Delhi, May 1917." In *The Location of Culture*, by Homi Bhabha, 102–22. London: Routledge, 1994d.

———. "The Third Space." In *Identity Community Culture Difference*, edited by Jonathon Rutherford, 207–21. London: Lawrence and Wishart, 1990b.

———. "Translator/Translated." *Artforum* (March 1995): 88–119.

Bilge, B., and Barbara Aswad, eds. Introduction. *Family and Gender among American Muslims: Issues Facing Middle Eastern Immigrants and Their Descendants*, edited by Bilge and Aswad, 1–13. Philadelphia: Temple University Press, 1996.

Brah, Avtar. *Cartographies of Diaspora: Contesting Identities*. London: Routledge, 1996.

Cainkar, Louise. "Palestinean-American Muslim Women: Living on the Margins of Two Worlds." In *Muslim Families in North America*, edited by Earle Waugh, Sharon McIrvin Abu-Laban, and Regula Qureshi, 282–308. Edmonton: University of Alberta Press, 1991.

Chatterjee, Pratha. *Nationalist Thought and the Colonial World: A Derivative Discourse*. Delhi: Oxford University Press, 1986.

Chatty, Habib. "Islam Finds Itself." In *The Islamic Impulse*, edited by Barbara Stowasser, 217–25. Washington, D.C.: Center for Contemporary Arab Studies, Georgetown University, 1987.

Chhachhi, Amrita. "The State, Religious Fundamentalism and Women: Trends in South Asia." *Economic and Political Weekly* 18 (March 1989): 567–78.

Claridge, Thomas. "Muslim Leader Loses Defamation Suit." *Globe and Mail* (June 1995): A7.

Corrigan, Philip. "Race/Ethnicity/Gender/Culture: Embodying Differences Educationally: An Argument." In *Breaking the Mosaic*, edited by Jon Young, 20–30. Toronto: Garamond, 1987.

Davis, Eric. "The Concept of Revival and the Study of Islam and Politics." In *The Islamic Impulse*, edited by B. Stowasser, 37–58. Washington, D.C.: Center for Contemporary Arab Studies, Georgetown University, 1987.

Dyer, Richard. *White*. London: Routledge, 1997.

El Guindi, F. "Veiling Infitah with Muslim Ethic: Egypt's Contemporary Islamic Movement." *Social Problems* 28, no. 4 (1981): 468–85.

Fanon, Frantz. *Black Skin White Masks*. New York: Grove Weidenfeld, 1967.

———. *A Dying Colonialism*. New York: Monthly Review Press, 1965.

Fleras, Augie, and Jean Elliott. "The Ethnic Experience." In *Unequal Relations: An Introduction to Race Ethnic and Aboriginal Dynamics in Canada*, by Augie Fleras and Jean Elliott, 160–86. Scarborough, Canada: Prentice Hall, 1996.

Freire, Paulo. *Pedagogy of the Oppressed*. New York: Seabury, 1968.

Gilroy, Paul. "The End of Anti-Racism." In *'Race,' Culture, and Difference*, edited by James Donald and Ali Rattansi, 49–61. London: Sage Publications, 1992.

Glazer, Nathan, and Daniel Moynihan. *Ethnicity: Theory and Experience*. Cambridge: Harvard University Press, 1975.

Goldberg, David T. *Anatomy of Racism*. Minneapolis: University of Minnesota Press, 1990.

Greenberg, M. F. *Marriage and Sexuality in Islam: A Translation of al-Ghazali's Book on the Etiquette of Marriage*. Salt Lake City: University of Utah Press, 1984.

Grossberg, L. "On Post-modernism and Articulation: An Interview with Stuart Hall." In *Stuart Hall: Critical Dialogues in Cultural Studies*, edited by D. Morley and K. Chen, 131–50. London: Routledge, 1996.

Haddad, Yvonne. "Maintaining the Faith of the Fathers: Dilemmas of Religious Identity in the Christian and Muslim Arab-American Communities." In *The Development of Arab-American Identity*, edited by Ernest McCarus, 61–84. Ann Arbor: University of Michigan Press, 1994.

Haddad, Yvonne, and Jane Smith. "Islamic Values among American Muslims." In *Family and Gender among American Muslims: Issues Facing Middle Eastern Immigrants and Their Descendants*, edited by Barbara Aswad and B. Bilge. Philadelphia: Temple University Press, 1996.

———. *Mission to America: Five Islamic Sectarian Communities in North America*. Gainesville: University Press of Florida, 1993.

Haeri, Shahla. *Law of Desire: Temporary Marriage in Shi'i*. Syracuse, N.Y.: Syracuse University Press, 1989.

Hall, Stuart. "Cultural Studies and Its Theoretical Legacies." In *Stuart Hall: Critical*

Dialogues in Cultural Studies, edited by D. Morley and K. Chen, 262–75. London: Routledge, 1996.

———. "New Ethnicities." In *Race, Culture, and Difference*, edited by James Donald and Ali Rattansi, 252–59. London: Sage Publications, 1992.

———. "Old and New Identities, Old and New Ethnicities." In *Culture, Globalization and the World-System: Contemporary Conditions for the Representation of Identity*, edited by Anthony King, 41–88. Minneapolis: University of Minnesota Press, 1997.

Harraway, Donna. "A Manifesto for Cyborgs: Science, Technology, and Socialist Feminism the Last Quarter." In *Women, Class, and the Feminist Imagination: A Socialist Feminist Reader*, edited by Karen V. Hansen and Irene S. Philpsim, 580–617. Philadelphia: Temple University Press, 1990.

Hasan, Farheen. "Young Muslim Women Redefining Feminism." *Varsity Opinion* 23 (November 1992): 2.

Haug, Frigga. *Female Sexualization*. London: Verso, 1987.

Helie-Lucas, Marie-Aimee. "The Preferential Symbol for Islamic Identity: Women in Muslim Personal Laws." In *Identity Politics and Women: Cultural Reassertions and Feminisms in International Perspective*, edited by Valentine Moghadam, 391–407. Boulder, Colo.: Westview, 1994.

Hoodfar, Homa. "The Veil in Their Minds and on Our Heads: The Persistence of Colonial Images of Muslim Women." *RFR* 22, nos. 3–4 (fall/winter 1993): 5–18.

hooks, bell. *Sisters of the Yam: Black Women and Self-Recovery*. Toronto: Between the Lines, 1993.

Hunter, S., ed. *The Politics of Islamic Revivalism*. Bloomington: Indiana University Press, 1988.

Kabani, Rana. *Europe's Myths of the Orient*. Bloomington: Indiana University Press, 1986.

Kandiyoti, Deniz, ed. Introduction. *Women, Islam and the State*, 1–21. Philadelphia: Temple University Press, 1991.

Kashmeri, Zuhair. *The Gulf Within: Canadian Arabs, Racism, and the Gulf War*. Toronto: James Lorimer, 1991.

Keating, Michael. "Two Faces under One Flag." *Times Higher Education Supplement* 24 (September 1993): 19.

Khalid, Detlev. "The Phenomenon of Re-Islamization." *Aussenpolitik* 29 (winter 1987): 433–53.

Khan, Shahnaz. "Influences Shaping Relations between the East Indians and the Anglo-Canadians in Canada: 1903–1947." *Journal of Ethnic Studies* 19, no. 1 (spring 1991): 101–15.

———. *Muslim Woman: Interrogating the Construct in Canada*. Ph.D. dissertation, University of Toronto (OISE), 1995a.

———. "Muslim Women and *Shari'a* Law: A Feminist Response to *Oh Canada*." *Canadian Journal of Women and the Law* 6, no. 1 (1993): 52–65.

———. "Race, Gender, and Orientalism: *Muta* and the Canadian Legal System." *Canadian Journal of Women and the Law* 8, no. 1 (1995b): 249–61.

————. "Representing Afghan Women." Manuscript.

————. "The Veil as a Site of Struggle: The *Hejab* in Quebec." *Canadian Women Studies* (spring/summer 1995c): 146–52.

Kirby, Sandra, and Kate McKenna. *Experience Research Social Change: Methods from the Margins.* Toronto: Garamond, 1989.

Kocturk, Tahire. *A Matter of Honour: Experiences of Turkish Women Immigrants.* N.p., N.J.: Zed, 1992.

Koran, The. N. J. Dawood, trans. Harmondsworth, England: Penguin, 1983.

Latif, Shahida. *Muslim Women in India: Political and Private Realities.* London: Zed, 1990.

Lavie, Smadar, and Ted Swedenburg, eds. *Displacement, Diaspora, and Geographies of Identity.* Durham, N.C.: Duke University Press, 1996.

Lawrence, Bruce. "Muslim Fundamentalist Movements: Reflections Towards a New Approach." In *The Islamic Impulse,* edited by B. Stowasser, 15–36. Washington, D.C.: Center for Contemporary Arab Studies, Georgetown University, 1987.

Lazreg, Marnia. "Feminism and Difference: The Perils of Writing as a Woman on Women in Algeria." In *Conflicts in Feminism,* edited by Marianne Hirsch and Evelyn Fox Keller, 326–48. New York: Routledge, 1990.

Lyotard, Jean François. *The Post-Modern Condition: A Report on Knowledge,* translated by Geof Bennington and Brian Massumi. Minneapolis: University of Minnesota Press, 1984.

Mabro, Judy. *Veiled Half-Truths: Western Travelers' Perceptions of Middle Eastern Women.* London: I. B. Tauris, 1991.

Margulies, Ronnie, and Ergin Yildizoglu. "The Political Uses of Islam in Turkey." *Middle East Report* (July/August 1988): 12–17.

McBratney, J. "Images of Indian Women in Rudyard Kipling: A Case of Doubling Discourse." *Inscriptions: Feminism and the Critique of Colonial Discourse* nos. 3–4 (1988): 47–58.

McIntosh, Peggy. "White Privilege: Unpacking the Invisible Knapsack." *Independent Schools* (winter 1990): 31–36.

Mernissi, Fatima. *Beyond the Veil: Male-Female Dynamics in Modern Muslim Society.* Bloomington: Indiana University Press, 1987.

Minh-Ha, Trinh. *Woman Native Other.* Bloomington: Indiana University Press, 1989.

Moghadam, Valentine. "Islamist Movements and Women's Responses in the Middle East." *Gender and History* 3, no. 3 (autumn 1991): 268–84.

Mohanty, Chandra. Introduction. *Third World Women and the Politics of Feminism,* edited by Chandra Mohanty, Ann Russo, and Lourdes Torres, 1–50. Bloomington: Indiana University Press, 1991a.

————. "Under Western Eyes: Feminist Scholarship and Colonial Discourses." In *Third World Women and the Politics of Feminism,* edited by Chandra Mohanty, Ann Russo, and Lourdes Torres, 51–80. Bloomington: Indiana University Press, 1991b.

Mojab, Shahrzad. "Islamic Feminism: Alternative or Contradiction." *Fireweed* (1995): 18–25.

Mumtaz, Khawar, and Farida Shaheed. *Women in Pakistan: Two Steps Forward One Step Back.* London: Zed, 1987.

Ng, Roxana. "Sexism, Racism, and Canadian Nationalism." In *Race, Class, Gender: Bonds and Barriers,* edited by Jesse Vorst, 10–25. Toronto: Between the Lines, 1989.

Ngugi, Wa Thiong'O. *Decolonizing the Mind.* London: Heinemann, 1989.

Patel, Pragna. "Review Essay: Alert for Action." *Feminist Review* 37 (spring 1991): 95–105.

Pennycook, Alistair. *The Cultural Politics of Teaching English in the World.* Ph.D. dissertation, University of Toronto (OISE), 1992.

Radhakrishnan, R. *Diasporic Mediations: Between Home and Location.* Minneapolis: University of Minnesota Press, 1996.

Rattansi, Ali. "Changing the Subject: Racism, Culture, and Education." In *Race, Culture, and Difference,* edited by James Donald and Ali Rattansi, 11–48. London: Sage Publications, 1992a.

———. Introduction. *Race, Culture and Difference,* edited by James Donald and Ali Rattansi, 1–10. London: Sage Publications, 1992b.

Roberts, L., and R. Clifton. "Multiculturalism in Canada: A Sociological Perspective." In *Multiculturalism in Canada,* edited by Augie Fleras and Jean Elliott, 120–47. Toronto: Nelson Canada, 1992.

Sabah, Fatna. *Woman in the Muslim Unconscious.* Oxford: Pergamon, 1984.

Sahgal, Gita, and Nira Yuval-Davis. *Refusing Holy Orders: Women and Fundamentalism in Britain.* London: Virago, 1992.

Said, Edward. *Covering Islam.* New York: Pantheon, 1981.

———. *Culture and Imperialism.* New York: Vintage, 1994.

———. *Orientalism.* London: Routledge and Kegan Paul, 1979.

Shaheen, Jack. *The TV Arab.* Bowling Green, Ohio: Popular Press, 1984.

Smith, Dorothy. *The Everyday World as Problematic.* Toronto: University of Toronto Press, 1987.

Smith, Julia Clancy. "The 'Passionate Nomad' Reconsidered: A European Woman *L'Algerie française* (Isabelle Eberhardt, 1877–1904)." In *Western Women and Imperialism: Complicity and Resistance,* edited by Nupur Chaudhuri and Margaret Strobel, 61–79. Bloomington: Indiana University Press, 1992.

Spivak, Gayatri. "Gayatri Spivak on the Politics of the Subaltern: Interview with Howard Winant." *Socialist Review* 20 (1990): 81–97.

———. *Outside in the Teaching Machine.* New York: Routledge, 1993.

Stephens, Julie. "Feminist Fictions: A Critique of the Category 'Non-Western Women' in Feminist Writings on Indian Women." In vol. 6 of *Subaltern Studies,* edited by Ranajit Guha, 92–131. Delhi: Oxford University Press, 1989.

Stowasser, Barbara. "Religious Ideology, Women, and the Family: The Islamic Paradigm." In *The Islamic Impulse,* edited by Stowasser, 262–96. Washington, D.C.: Center for Contemporary Arab Studies, Georgetown University, 1987.

Strobel, Margaret, and Nupur Chaudhuri. Introduction. *Western Women and Imperialism: Complicity and Resistance,* edited by Nupur Chaudhuri and Margaret Strobel. Bloomington: Indiana University Press, 1992.

Suleri, Sara. *Meatless Days.* Chicago: University of Chicago Press, 1987.

Tibi, Basam. "Islam and Nationalism." In *The Islamic Impulse,* edited by Barbara Stowasser, 59–74. Washington, D.C.: Center for Contemporary Arab Studies, Georgetown University, 1987.

Torres, Lourdes. "The Construction of the Self in U.S. Latina Autobiographies." In *Third World Women and the Politics of Feminism,* edited by Chandra Mohanty, Ann Russo, and Lourdes Torres, 271–87. Bloomington: Indiana University Press, 1991a.

Waugh, Earle, Sharon McIrvin Abu-Laban, and R. Qureshi, eds. *Muslim Families in North America.* Edmonton: University of Alberta Press, 1991.

Yuval-Davis, Nira. *Gender and Nation.* London: Sage Publications, 1997.

———. "Identity Politics and Women's Ethnicity." In *Identity Politics and Women's Cultural Reassertions and Feminisms in International Perspective,* edited by Valentine Moghadam, 408–24. Boulder, Colo.: Westview, 1994.

INDEX

Shahnaz Khan is an assistant professor of women's studies and sociology at St. Francis Xavier University, Antigonish, Nova Scotia, Canada. She is the author of numerous articles on Muslim women and immigration in such journals as *Signs: Journal of Women in Culture and Society* and *Journal of Ethnic Studies*.